DISCARD

THE ARCHER'S BIBLE
Revised Edition

THE ARCHER'S BIBLE

Revised Edition

Fred Bear

Doubleday

New York London Toronto Sydney Auckland

Published by Doubleday, a division of
Bantam Doubleday Dell Publishing Group, Inc.,
666 Fifth Avenue, New York, New York 10103

Doubleday and the portrayal of an anchor with a dolphin
are trademarks of Doubleday, a division of
Bantam Doubleday Dell Publishing Group, Inc.

Library of Congress Cataloging in Publication Data

Bear, Fred.
   The archer's bible.

   1. Archery. 2. Hunting with bow and arrow.
I. Title.
GV1185.B34   1980   799.2′15
ISBN: 0-385-15155-1
Library of Congress Catalog Card Number 79–7585

    15   17   19   20   18   16   14

BG

CONTENTS

LURE OF THE BOW

Archery can certainly be described as "the sport of man since time began." When present-day archers take up the bow and arrow for fun and recreation, their satisfaction comes from a skill almost as old as human existence itself.

Though it is impossible to date precisely the invention of the bow and arrow, many historians agree that the development of archery, along with the harnessing of fire and the invention of language, was a critical factor in man's rise above his fellow creatures. In those early days, and indeed for many centuries thereafter, the bow was a tool of grim necessity in obtaining food and winning battles.

For more than five thousand years of recorded history, the bow has played an extremely important role in human affairs. Many nations, in fact whole societies (among them, the Egyptians, Sumerians, Greeks, Romans, Babylonians, Syrians, Turks, Persians, Arabians, Mongols, Chinese, and Japanese), have risen or fallen on flights of humming arrow shafts. Inevitably, the bow and arrow made their way into the myths and legends of many civilizations: Among the legendary (and historical) archer heroes are Odysseus, the Amazons, Genghis Khan, Tamerlane, Sultan Saladin, Robin Hood, and our own Hiawatha, to name but a few.

With the development and perfection of firearms, archery lost its importance in warfare, yet it retained its popularity in many parts of the world as a sporting and hunting arm. Indeed, as the romantic sport *par excellence,* archery still appeals to man's atavistic instincts. It gives him the chance to relive subconsciously the exploits of his warrior ancestors, who conquered enemies and sustained life with little else than their bow and arrows.

There are, however, many more practical reasons behind the great popularity of archery today. It is a fun, family sport that can be played individually or in groups by people of both sexes and all ages. It is easy to learn, relatively inexpensive, and offers a large variety of games for every level of proficiency; it can also be as leisurely or competitive as one chooses. Many sports largely exclude women, but archery imposes no such limitation. Sheer strength is not a prerequisite to success, and women not only can excel in the sport but find it to be an extremely good builder of posture and poise. And needless to say, archery is a great way to develop physical fitness.

Some archery fans limit their activities to target shooting. They develop skill and enjoy the camaraderie afforded by family outings or competitive shoots. Others go further and use the bow and arrow for hunting; they pit their skill against game on a more equal basis than is possible with a gun.

If you are one of the millions who have discovered archery, it is our hope that you will find information of value in this book. If you are not yet a bowman or bowwoman, this book may help you to understand the very real lure of the sport. A word of caution, however: The archery bug is catching! The chances are great that once you see the fun it offers, you won't be satisfied until you, too, are regularly enjoying the twang of the bowstring and the swish of your own well-sped arrows.

Archery is one of the finest of all sports for participation by the entire family. (Browning Arms Company Photo.)

Chapter 1

SELECTION OF EQUIPMENT

If the beginner in archery is to experience the progress that makes for lasting interest and maximum enjoyment, he or she must begin with properly fitted equipment.

It is not wise to attempt to outfit yourself and family on your own. Seeking out a qualified expert in this respect will save you much time and confusion. There are four major sources of such professional help. By far the best is the sporting-goods dealer who specializes in archery tackle or who employs a knowledgeable clerk to run his archery department. Such stores stock a variety of tackle and often have a place where customers can actually try it out. They can quickly settle questions that come up concerning proper matching of the various components and can help with small services such as repairs and replacement of tackle items.

A second source of help are the indoor archery lanes. These are not so widespread as organized archery clubs but are available in many parts of the country. The lanes normally contain a pro shop and an experienced archer or archers in charge who will let you try out various bows on the premises.

Third, advice in choosing bows and other equipment can be found in the local archery club. The more experienced and proficient members are always willing to help a beginner. But ask advice of more than one archer. Some of them, in common with trout fishermen and golfers, develop prejudices in tackle selection and use items which may be right for them but not so good for the average archer or beginner. Asking help of

two or three such experts will usually give you a much better idea of how to start. Again, membership in a club offers the advantage of familiarizing yourself with equipment before buying it.

For those who live in small rural communities where none of the above sources of help is available, the best alternative is correspondence with one of the reputable archery manufacturers. By stating your age, height, weight, general physical condition and preference for type of archery participation (backyard, target, field, bowhunting, or some combination of these), you can obtain specific recommendations which lack only the opportunity to actually test-shoot the tackle.

CHOOSING A BOW

To those interested in becoming archers or bowhunters, a primary consideration is of course the proper choice of a bow. This choice is often confusing to the beginner, chiefly because the types and brands of archery tackle have considerably increased with the ever-growing demand. Present-day bows vary in length from 4 to 6 feet or more. In general, the shorter bows are used for hunting, particularly from blinds or in brushy country, while the longer ones are used for target or tournament shooting. For all-around use, a bow of medium length, say between 5 and 5½ feet, is best for the average man, woman, or youngster.

When buying an initial bow of any type other than a compound, it is a good rule to find a bow that you can easily hold at full draw for ten seconds and then purchase one five pounds heavier. The reason for this is that the back and shoulder muscles used in drawing a bow develop rapidly with practice; thus you "work into" a heavier bow within a relatively short time.

Bow weight, incidentally, does not pertain to the actual weight of the bow but rather to the drawing force, measured in pounds, necessary to draw an arrow to its full length. Practically all bowyers have standardized their bow weights at 28 inches of draw, simply because the arm span of most adult men is suited to this arrow length. Bows are usually marked by manufacturers with the weight required to pull this arrow length.

Special scales used by archery manufacturers to establish the correct drawing weight of each bow.

Not all archers of course use a 28-inch arrow, and it is obvious that a person with a 26-inch draw will be drawing less weight, while one with a 30-inch draw will be increasing the draw weight. In most makes of bows this loss or gain in draw weight will be about 2 to 2½ pounds for every inch the draw is shortened or lengthened. Instructions for determining an individual's proper draw length (arrow length) will be found in the following section on arrows.

Beginners should avoid the use of overly heavy bows. There is nothing so disheartening as struggling with a bow which is too heavy for one's strength. It will result in poor shooting habits, loss of accuracy, and often a loss of interest in

the sport before one really gets started. The fault of "overbowing" is particularly prevalent among those purchasing a bow for hunting use.

In years past, bowhunters commonly used bows pulling 60 to 70 pounds and more. They had to use that draw weight to get the penetration needed from the all-wood bows of that day. Now the tremendous improvements in bow design and materials have changed all this. Records compiled by the various State Conservation and Fish & Game Departments show that the overall national average for hunting bow weights falls be-

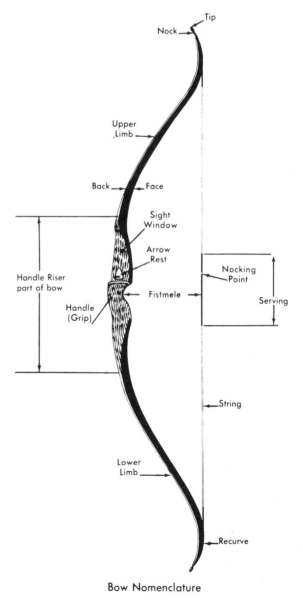

Bow Nomenclature

(Browning Arms Company.)

tween 45 and 55 pounds. This weight range in our modern bows is entirely sufficient for hunting all but the largest game and yet is not too tiring for use by the average man for practice.

The best method by far of fitting an individual with a bow is for him to draw bows of the general weight recommended for his age group. This is particularly helpful since individuals of similar size, especially women, vary a great deal in strength.

The following table gives a general draw-weight guide as a starting point.

Small children	10 – 15 lbs.
Ten to twelve years	15 – 20 lbs.
Teenage girls and women	20 – 30 lbs.
Teenage boys and men	30 – 40 lbs.
Beginning hunting bows for men	40 – 55 lbs.

NOTES ON BOW DESIGN

Desirable qualities in bows result from applying certain fundamental laws of physics. One is the basic fact that light objects are easier to move than heavy ones. This applies particularly to the limbs of a bow which should be as light as possible but still amply strong for the job they must do. Lightness in the bow limbs makes possible their rapid acceleration and at the same time

minimizes jar or recoil from the sudden shock that occurs when the limbs are stopped by the bowstring. It is interesting to note that on release from full draw the ends of the bow limbs travel through an arc of less than 8 inches.

The handle section, or "riser," of modern target bows, on the other hand, is often fairly heavy. Some present bow models have a total actual weight in excess of 4 pounds, practically all of which is in the long riser. Tournament shooters like this added weight because it affords extra stability and deadens vibration of the limbs so that none of the jar from releasing is transmitted to the bow arm.

It is a different matter with hunting bows. In them, the handle section is much lighter than in target bows. To the bowhunter, ease of carrying and velocity of arrows are more important than the stability needed for "nock splitting."

When the word "bow" is mentioned, it is natural to think of wood. Today, however, composite or laminated construction has all but replaced the wood bow.

Solid-glass bows are quite popular in the lower-price brackets. Their chief advantage, other than low cost, is ruggedness—they can stand a great deal of abuse. On the other hand, they do not shoot as smoothly and do not have

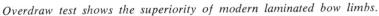

Overdraw test shows the superiority of modern laminated bow limbs.

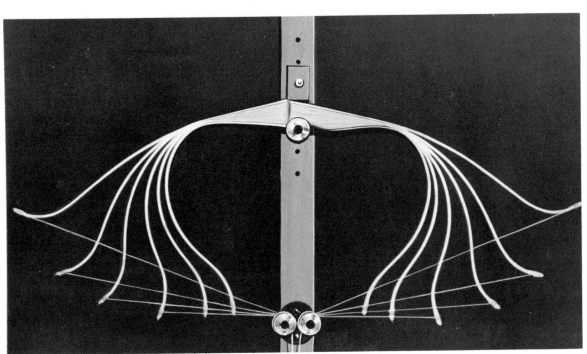

the cast per draw weight of composite bows.

The most efficient bow-limb design yet developed employs fiber glass, a high-tensile and compressive-strength material, on the outside surfaces (back and face) and a tough lightweight material such as maple for the center, or core, laminations.

The great majority of present-day conventional bows have recurved rather than straight limbs. (Modern conventional-bow construction is actually an adaptation of designs used by ancient Turkish and Persian bowyers, who achieved outstanding results with their recurved composite bows.) Recurving the limb ends has the effect of making the limb, or lever, longer as the bow approaches full draw, thus storing additional energy. This not only makes the bow easier to draw but results in better cast, which simply means that such a bow will shoot an arrow faster and farther than one with poor cast. Recurved bows have greater cast in any given draw weight than straight-limbed bows.

Since recurved bows have come into general use, tournament scores have improved fantastically and bowhunters have noted a marked improvement in their sport as well.

Most otherwise straight bows are made with the limbs slightly reflexed. Recurved bows (ends curved away from the shooter) are generally somewhat reflexed also. In some designs both the reflex and deflex principles are employed along with recurved ends. These are called duoflex. But whatever the limb design, recurved bows have better cast and are smoother to shoot than nonrecurved ones.

Almost all bows today have formed, comfortable handles. They are also cut away to allow the arrow to pass near the center of the bow. This cutout section is elongated both to provide room for a bowsight if desired and to give the shooter a clearer view of the target.

Whatever type or make of bow you choose initially, start with a medium-weight model and get the best you can afford. In archery, as in all other sports, you will get the best results from the best equipment.

THE COMPOUND BOW

Comparatively new in the field of archery equipment is the compound bow. As is often the case with radical innovations, it is a controversial item. Many think of it as the greatest archery concept since laminated limbs, while others have claimed it is a mere mechanical device destined to ruin the sport. The controversy surrounding the compound does not stem from its performance, which is excellent, but rather from its appearance. It is odd-looking and considerably different from the clean, flowing, uncluttered lines of the traditional bow.

The typical compound bow has short, stiff limbs. It can consist of one full-length piece or two separate limbs joined to a handle section. Eccentric wheels at the limb ends, either in metal bracket extensions or in the slotted limb tips, may be accompanied by additional wheels and pulleys mounted on the limbs, with a series of cables connecting these to the bowstring.

The idea of the compound bow is not new. Dr. Claude J. Lapp, a physicist in Washington, D.C., designed the first one prior to 1940. It performed very well, but its strangeness did not meet with favor and Dr. Lapp shelved the idea. It wasn't until the mid-1960s that H. W. Allen of Billings, Missouri, developed the first commercial models. In 1967 he produced fewer than 100 compounds, only to find they were frequently banned from archery competition.

As more bows were produced and more archers had the opportunity to try them, the compound gradually gained acceptance. The National Field Archery Association sanctioned its use for both competition and bowhunting, although as yet it is still not approved for national or international target competition by the N.A.A., F.I.T.A., and P.A.A. Its fast-growing popularity and widespread use, however, may bring about a change in the rulings within the foreseeable future.

What is so exciting about this radical design? The answer lies in that ungraceful but efficient system of eccentric wheels and cables. In a conventional bow, the drawing weight continues to increase as the string is drawn, right up to full draw. In the compound, the drawing weight peaks at mid-draw, then decreases as you reach full draw, the reduction being as much as 50 percent in some models.

It is not difficult to understand this advantage. On a fifty-pound bow the holding weight is 25 pounds at a 50 percent dropoff. This gives a major increase in foot-pounds of energy for ap-

Examples of rope/spike- and trigger-release aids.

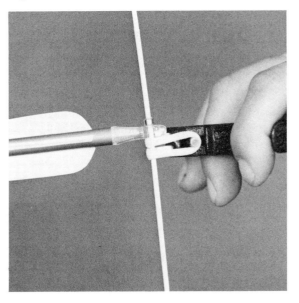

Proper positioning of rope/spike-release aid. These are often used in place of a glove or tab by competitive archers using a compound bow.

plication to the arrow and provides a more relaxed aiming time.

These bows also propel an arrow at a somewhat greater velocity, and lighter weight arrows can be used to obtain additional velocity, which is an advantage in providing a flatter trajectory. It is wrong, however, to use lightweight arrows for hunting as they lack the striking energy required for big game.

Lighter-weight bows require a much cleaner or crisper release of the arrow for good accuracy, and this problem presents itself in the compound bow with its greatly lessened holding weight.

During the same period that the compound bow became popular, another item was developed—the release aid. This comes in various forms: the solid one-piece, the pivoting ledge, the trigger, and the rope-spike, but all are similar in use and effect, i.e., better accuracy in shooting.

However, the beginner should initially learn with a glove or tab on the release hand (hand drawing the bowstring), as shooting in this fashion is easier and more natural to begin with than using a mechanically activated release aid. The purpose of either the shooting glove or tab is to

Former N.F.A.A. National Champion, Ron Lauhon, shows proper form with the release aid. (Jennings Archery photo.)

protect the fingers of the drawing hand from the pressure of the bowstring when the bow is drawn. Release aids are a bit more complicated but make it possible to hold and draw the bow without the fingers being in contact with the bowstring. As releases are more sophisticated they can add confusion to the many things one must remember in shooting a bow. They are not generally used for hunting, nor have they as yet been sanctioned for national or international tournament use. Perhaps, like bowsights and stabilizers,

they will eventually be accepted. In the meantime, although the compound bow can certainly be shot effectively using a glove or tab, for target use many archers have resorted to one of the release aids now on the market.

Most present compounds can be classified as either 2-wheelers or 4-wheelers, although there are models that use additional idler pulleys or synchronizing wheels. There are no hard-and-fast rules about which arrangement is best. 4-wheelers are considered the most versatile compounds, yet 2-wheelers have the potential for high efficiency, are less complicated, and generally cost less.

As a starting point, the 4-wheeler is usually chosen for top target performance while the 2-wheeler is excellent for hunting. There are many good models available, as evidenced by the major share they hold of the present bow market. New developments along this line in the years ahead will be interesting to follow.

MATCHING ARROWS

Good arrows, properly matched to the user's arm length and to the draw weight of his bow, are perhaps the single most important item of an archer's tackle.

Modern arrows are made of three basic materials: wood, glass, and metal. The metal arrows, made of aluminum-alloy tubing, are used principally by target and tournament archers. They are supreme as precision instruments.

Wood arrows are made of birch, fir, and some types of pine and cedar. Port Orford cedar, found only in a few coastal counties of southern Oregon and northern California, has long been the most popular and widely used shaft material. Arrows made from this wood are reasonable in price and yet can be obtained in sets matched quite closely in weight and spine.

Glass arrows are comparatively new, although some brands have been on the market for many years. They are quite rugged and will stand a lot of abuse under field-shooting or hunting conditions and remain straight. They will stand almost any amount of bending up to the breaking point and still retain their original straightness.

While wood shafts still dominate the field in hunting arrows, constant improvement in glass and aluminum shaft construction is making the latter materials more and more popular. In price, glass arrows are intermediate: more expensive than wood but less expensive than metal.

Beginners usually start with wood arrows. Since they are less expensive, the loss is not so great when one is lost or broken. After the archer has enough shooting experience to keep his arrows on or close to the target, he can then invest in the more expensive and efficient glass or aluminum arrows.

Use of light draw-check bow to determine proper arrow length.

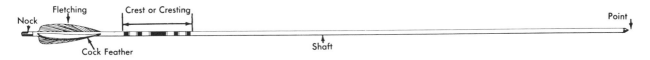

Arrow Nomenclature

(*Browning Arms Company.*)

MATCHING TO DRAW LENGTHS

Although bow weight is usually marked on the basis of a 28-inch draw, this does not mean that arrows must be of that length to shoot in such a bow. Correct arrow length, which is determined by the arm span of the archer, is a very important factor in archery. If the arrow is too short, there is danger of overdrawing, with possible injury to the hand holding the bow or to the bow itself. If too long, the extra length will add weight and result in loss of speed and flat trajectory.

The easiest and most accurate way to determine your arrow length is to draw a long arrow in a lightweight bow and hold it at your anchor point while someone marks the shaft with a pencil at the point where it crosses the leading edge of the bow. Correct draw length for target or practice arrows will be the measurement from this mark to the bottom of the nock slot.

An alternate method of finding the arrow length best suited to you is to have someone measure across your outspread arms from fingertip to fingertip and then refer to the following table:

ARM SPREAD	ARROW LENGTH
57 – 59″	22 – 23″
60 – 62″	23 – 24″
63 – 65″	24 – 25″
66 – 68″	25 – 26″
69 – 71″	26 – 27″
72 – 74″	27 – 28″
75 – 77″	28 – 29″
over 77″	30 – 32″

The average modern glass-laminated bow will lose or gain approximately 2 to 2½ pounds in draw weight for every inch the draw is shortened or lengthened. This means that if you use a 26-inch arrow and buy a bow marked 45 pounds (at 28 inches), you will actually be drawing about 40 pounds.

As can be seen in the diagram on the following page, extra length (usually ¾ inch) is included on hunting shafts to provide room for full draw without touching the fingers of the bow hand with the broadhead. In the excitement of hunting, an arrow is sometimes slightly overdrawn and the extra length protects the archer's bow hand from possible contact with the sharp broadhead. If your draw length happens to be 27 inches for regular target arrows, you would also order 27-inch hunting arrows, but with the understanding that they would actually be 27¾ inches to the back of the head. Field or hunting practice arrows are made with the same extra length in order to more nearly match the hunting arrows in performance. Bowfishing arrows also have extra length—again, for the safety factor.

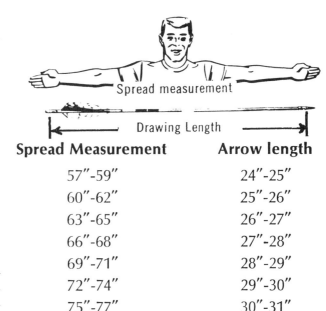

Spread Measurement	Arrow length
57″-59″	24″-25″
60″-62″	25″-26″
63″-65″	26″-27″
66″-68″	27″-28″
69″-71″	28″-29″
72″-74″	29″-30″
75″-77″	30″-31″

Alternate arm-spread measurement.

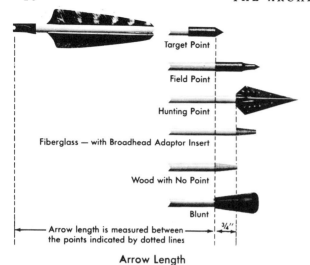

Target Point

Field Point

Hunting Point

Fiberglass — with Broadhead Adaptor Insert

Wood with No Point

Blunt

← Arrow length is measured between → ¾"
the points indicated by dotted lines

Arrow Length

(*Browning Arms Company.*)

Incidentally, when choosing arrows for very young archers it is far better to buy them too long than too short. For youngsters, safety outweighs exacting results.

The majority of arrows are fitted with fletching —three feathers or plastic vanes—to guide them. (Actually, turkey-wing feathers, the traditional fletching material, have been largely replaced today by plastic vanes.) One feather is always set on the shaft at right angles to the slot of the nock and is usually a different color from the other two. This is called the "cock feather," while the other two are referred to as "hen feathers." The feathers are fastened on the shaft at a slight angle or spiral to make the arrow rotate in flight and thus travel straight—a function comparable to that performed by the rifling grooves in a gun barrel. Some archers use four feathers, or vanes, instead of three, but this is more or less a matter of personal taste.

MATCHING TO BOW WEIGHT

In order to perform properly, arrows must be matched in spine (i.e., the stiffness of the shaft) to the draw weight of your bow. When an arrow is released, it bends around the bow handle before straightening out in full flight. If the arrow shaft is not of the correct stiffness, or spine, it will bend either too little or too much and thus be thrown off course. Arrows that are too stiff for the bow's drawing weight may not bend enough and will therefore fly off to the left. Arrows that are too limber are even more erratic and may fly

off either to the right or left. If in doubt when choosing between different sets of arrows, choose the ones with the stiffer spine.

When ordering arrows from a manufacturer, the archer should give the draw length, the weight of the bow the arrows are for, and the type of head or point wanted. With this information the manufacturer can furnish arrows with shafts of the correct spine to match the customer's needs. All reliable manufacturers mark this information on the outside of the arrow carton. By saving this information the archer can later reorder arrows to match the previous set.

Two bows may have exactly the same draw weights, yet one may have much more cast or shoot an arrow faster and farther than the other. The faster bow will require a stiffer arrow than the more sluggish one. The old English longbow design, with a handle section an inch or more wide at the arrow pass, called for an arrow spine matched very closely to the bow's draw weight, as the shaft had the full width of bow to bend around before it could resume straight flight. Modern bows are much closer to being "center shot" and are thus more tolerant of spine variation. Many archers have found that if arrows are not perfectly matched to the bow, they can still get good flight with them by widening the bow-handle section at the arrow plate. Just an added $\frac{1}{16}$ inch often makes a surprising difference in

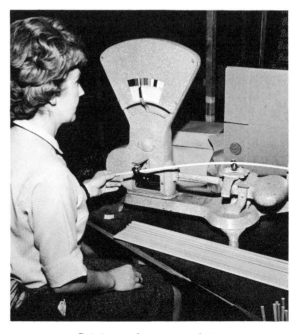

Spining cedar arrow shafts.

Applying the fletching to arrows.

how the arrows fly. Up to ¼ inch may be necessary for your shooting form. A few manufacturers cut in the sight window slightly beyond center and install an adjustable arrow rest. The archer can thus "tune" his bow for perfect arrow take-off.

In any dozen matched arrows, the weight should not vary much. However, in several dozens matched in spine for identical bow weights, the weight may vary considerably. This is especially true of wood shafts but is really of little consequence.

For glass and aluminum arrows the manufacturers can furnish detailed charts for matching shaft sizes and spines to the various bow weights. Serious archers should obtain copies of these charts for ready reference.

All types of arrows can be used with a compound bow provided they are properly matched to it in spine. As with any conventional bow, properly matched arrows are more important than the bow itself for achieving best results. Arrows should be selected to match the peak weight of your compound.

Nowadays most archers—particularly top target and field archers—shoot arrows that are well matched to their bows. However, there is still room for improvement in hunting arrows. In some areas lighter hunting bows are being used than was formerly the rule. Archers shooting

these comparatively light bows often make the mistake of using the lightest arrow that will fly correctly from the bow, in the hope of flattening the arrow's trajectory. However, at the average bowhunting range (20 to 40 yards), the factor of trajectory is not too important. More important is obtaining maximum striking power. A heavy hunting arrow absorbs greater energy from the bow than does a light one, and while it may fly a bit slower, it will hit harder and afford better penetration. In addition, the extra weight of the broadhead point will be better balanced on a heavy shaft. Target-weight shafts are too light to be properly balanced with the heavier hunting heads.

Fletching on hunting arrows must be larger than on target arrows. The larger feathers, or vanes, are necessary to counterbalance the heavier shaft and broadhead and thus provide adequate steering in flight. Hunting fletch should always be applied in a helical spiral. Spiraled feathers spin the arrow in flight and keep it on a straight course.

Blunt points are used on arrows intended for practice and for hunting small game such as rabbits and squirrels, but broadheads, with very sharp cutting edges, should be used for hunting all game from the size of woodchucks on up. Further notes on hunting arrows of various types will be found in the bowhunting chapters.

Always buy arrows from a reliable source and get the best you can afford. The results will be worth the cost.

BASIC ACCESSORY TACKLE

Three items of equipment other than the bow and arrows are basic necessities: the arm guard, or bracer; the shooting glove, or tab; and the quiver, or arrow carrier. Several other items are very helpful, and various refinements are available to suit individual needs.

The arm guard is usually made of leather, although less-expensive plastic models are also used. Some of the better leather guards have steel stays sewn inside to help them retain their shape. The arm guard is worn on the inside of the forearm that holds the bow. Its purpose is to protect the arm and wrist from the occasional sting of the bowstring when an arrow is released. The arm guard is most useful when worn over a shirt or jacket sleeve, as it confines the material close to the arm where it won't interfere with the bowstring. A good leather arm guard costs about $3 or $4. Plastic models run a dollar or two less.

Finger protection for the drawing hand, if a release aid is not used, can be obtained by using either a shooting glove or a shooting tab. The tab is inexpensive (from $1 to $2) and is somewhat like a mitten with the back cut away. It takes some getting used to because it does not fit over the fingers as a glove does, but it gives a very clean release. Many top target and professional archers use the tab.

For beginners, for the casual archer, and for the bowhunter, a shooting glove is usually recommended because, unlike the tab, it is always firmly set in place on the fingers. It is actually the skeleton of a glove, with but three finger stalls for the first three fingers of the drawing hand. The finger stalls can be made of either soft cowhide or firm steer or cordovan leather. The choice is up to the individual: some archers prefer to feel the pressure of the bowstring while others, with more sensitive skin, need the extra protection of the heavier leather. When selecting a new glove, get one which fits the fingers snugly. A little use will stretch the leather somewhat and conform it comfortably to the hand. Any new glove needs some use before it gets that "just right" feel. The best way to break in a new shooting glove is to soak it

in water and shoot with it wet. Once broken in, a good shooting glove will last for years.

One excellent type of glove features detachable finger stalls, which means you can select a perfectly fitting stall for each finger and then attach them to a glove back of the right length for an ideal fit. Shooting gloves are priced between $3 and $5.

The third essential accessory is the quiver. Available in many variations, all of which have advantages, the simplest and least expensive quiver is the pocket type, which holds a half-dozen target or field-tipped arrows. Pocket quivers are excellent for the casual backyard shooter or for use on the field range.

Belt quivers hang from the side over the hip and hold from six to twenty arrows. They are used chiefly by target archers. One of the latest quiver models is the "holster" type, which combines the best features of both side and hip quivers. It fastens to the belt, carries six or more arrows, and has a tie-down leg thong. These are currently popular among field archers.

Back quivers are perhaps the oldest form of arrow carrier and are especially popular with youngsters both because of their capacity (one to three dozen arrows) and their association with

An arm guard should always be worn to prevent possible abrasion of the arm by the bowstring.

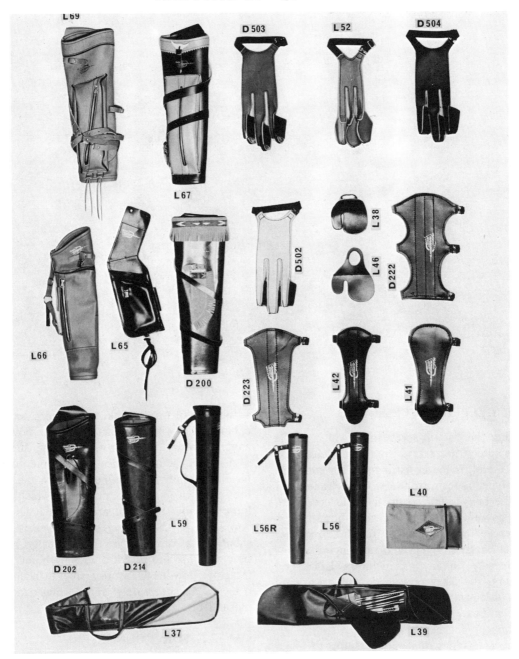

Leather archery accessories. (Shakespeare Company Photo.)

ancient Indian warriors. One type of back quiver hangs at an angle across the back with the arrows protruding over the shoulder; another hangs down the center of the back by means of a pack-style harness.

Back quivers are not often used by target shooters, but many bowhunters use them, and archers who shoot field courses, in preparation for hunting, use them to accustom themselves to drawing arrows out rapidly when needed.

Specialized quiver variations are made strictly for hunting. These will be discussed in the chapter on bowhunting.

Bow-pal cord-type bow-stringer in use. (Schwartz Studios, Inc.)

OTHER HELPFUL ACCESSORIES

Heading the list of accessories, which, while not absolutely necessary, are nevertheless extremely useful, is the bowstringer. This comes in various types ranging from a wooden frame over which the bow is braced, to a single cord with leather bow-tip holders. The cord bowstringers are an exceedingly handy item for three reasons: (a) They make stringing and unstringing a bow easy and safe for anyone, including ladies and youngsters. (b) They prevent damage to a good bow by doing away with limb twisting. And (c) they weigh but a few ounces and can be carried in the archer's pocket.

Other accessories that are helpful to most archers are a bow case for transporting and storing the bow in style and safety; nocking points to insure correct arrow placement on the string; bowstring wax to prolong the life of a good string; a stringkeeper to hold proper brace height of string and protect upper bow nock when bow is unstrung, a storage rack to hold bows correctly when not in use; and last but not least, an extra bowstring for every bow.

A storage rack can be anything from wall hooks on which bows are hung vertically by the string loop or upper nock, to the more decorative cabinet type, which holds three to six bows horizontally on pegs, plus arrows and other tackle.

A few of the accessories which come under the heading of individual refinements are the following: a shirt or blouse protector which shields loose clothing from the arrow and bowstring, a bowsight for those interested in precise target shooting, a bow square to correctly measure brace heights and position nocking points, shooting-glove powder to insure a smooth release, and a tackle case for safely transporting a dozen or more arrows and other accessories.

TACKLE FOR YOUNGSTERS

Children like to have the feeling of belonging, and in archery they can do just that. They can be a part of the same group or club as their parents and do the same things at the same time, combining healthful exercise and comradeship with discipline and competitive spirit. Children can begin in family groups at five or six years of age. Usually, however, a child is nine or ten years old before he or she takes an active interest in the sport.

Many leading archery manufacturers offer

tackle tailored especially to the needs of young people. For the very young—say, from five or six years up to ten—complete archery sets are available at $10 or less. Such sets center around a solid fiber-glass bow of a length and draw weight suitable to the age group.

For boys and girls a bit older—from ten to seventeen—complete sets, including a laminated recurve bow "just like Dad's," are available. Such sets usually run between $20 and $30. For those who do not want a complete set, a bow in the $15–$20 class and a dozen matched wood arrows, plus tab or glove, arm guard, and quiver, would be a sensible starting point.

No bow and arrow should be classified as a toy. Any of the metal-tipped points used on target or field arrows can be lethal, even when released from a very light bow. This means that youngsters must be supervised when using archery tackle, and the rules of safety should be drilled into them before they get the chance to experiment on their own. The basic rule is the same as for firearms: Never aim an arrow at anything you don't want to shoot.

Children have a keen desire to shoot arrows straight up in the air "to see how high they will go." This practice must be discouraged. Urge them, instead, to enjoy the low arching flight of an arrow and be sure they have plenty of open space to do so.

Competent instruction in shooting fundamentals, plus constant drilling in safety rules, is the only safe way to start off a boy or girl in archery. The right start will lead to a lifetime of enjoyment.

Shirt, or blouse, protector and extra-long arm guard keep loose clothing out of the path of the bowstring.

PANEL OF BEGINNER BOWS

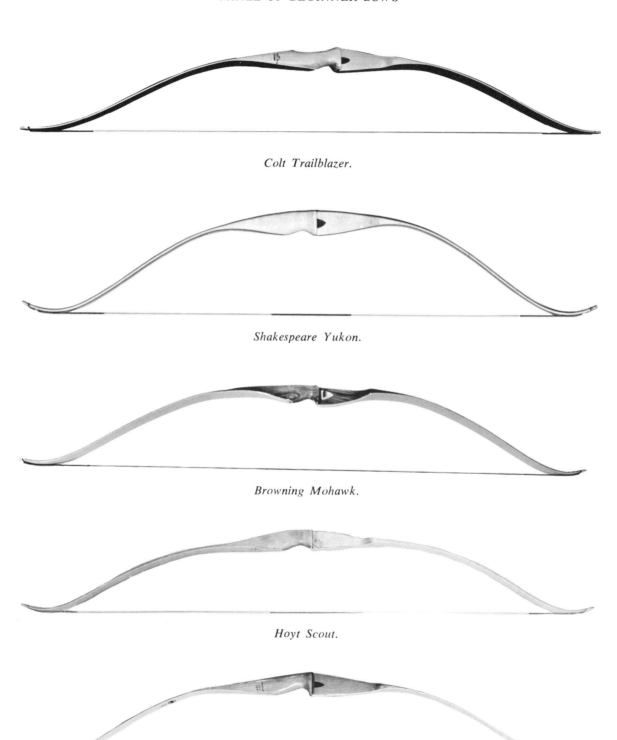

Colt Trailblazer.

Shakespeare Yukon.

Browning Mohawk.

Hoyt Scout.

Bear Cub. (Stedman Studio.)

The quality beginner bows shown here are all less than $30 in price.

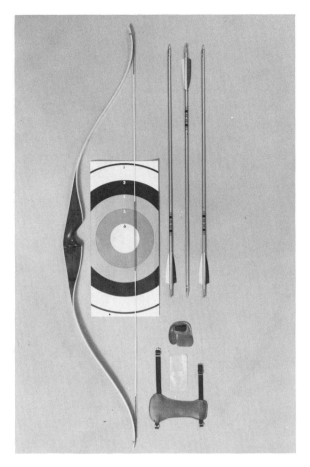

Bear Little Bear Set

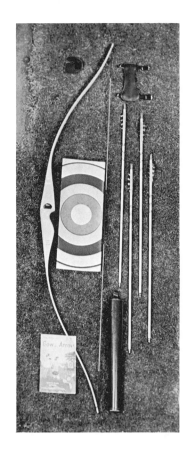

Bear Cub Set. (Stedman Studio.)

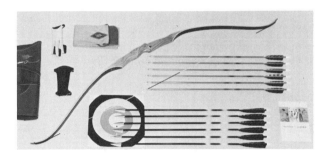
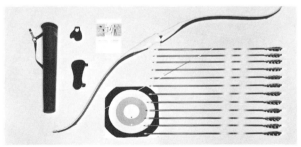

Shakespeare medium-priced sets.

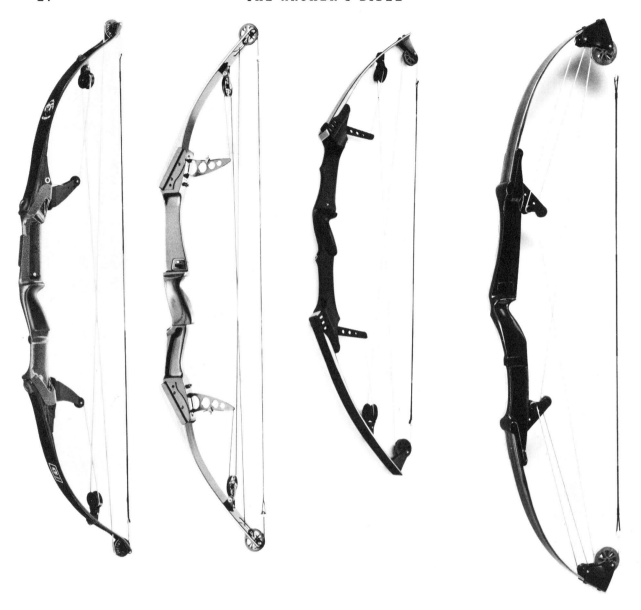

Four-wheel compound bows. These are the most complex designs, featuring very fine tuning adjustments, a wide degree of peak adjustment, and maximum arrow velocity.

Chapter II

FOUNDATIONS OF GOOD SHOOTING

PRELIMINARY STEPS

Before attempting to master the principles of good shooting form, one should first learn the necessary preliminaries to actual shooting of the bow. The first of these is correct stringing or bracing of the bow, without harming it or yourself.

BRACING THE BOW

There are only two safe ways to brace a bow. By far the best and simplest of these is the use of a bowstringing device, which comes in a variety of styles. The larger wood device is handy for family use in backyard shooting or for archery-club members shooting either indoors or out. The lighter pocket-size cord stringers (see page 20) are ideal for individual use.

A cord stringer is a length of strong nylon with end pockets of leather. With the lower bowstring loop in place on the lower nock and the upper loop slipped on over the bow limb, the end pockets of the bowstringer are fitted over the bow tips. It is then a simple matter to stand on the center of the cord, pull the bow up at the handle, and slip the upper string loop into the nock. A cord bowstringer is one of the best $3–$4 investments in archery tackle you can possible make, especially if you are new to the sport.

For those who start out without a bowstringer, or who prefer to string a bow by hand, there is only one really safe method of stringing. It is called the "step-across" method and is accomplished as follows: First, the string loop should

be in place on the lower bow nock and held in place by a rubber band or a bow-tip protector. Holding the other string loop in the left hand, step across the bow with your right leg so that the bow handle lies against the back of your thigh, as high up as possible. Your right leg is between the bow and the bowstring. The pressure of the thigh must be against the bow handle to avoid bending one limb more than the other. Hold the upper bow limb just under the recurve in your right

Step-across method of bowstringing.

Eyes on String
Alignment over
Lower Recurve

Bow Handle
High Up
Under Buttock

Apply Pressure
Against Recurve
Not Against End
of Bow

Heel Raised

hand and place the lower recurve over the instep of your left foot, being careful not to let the bow tip touch the floor or ground. (Some archers use a leather harness slipped on over the shoe to hold the bow tip in the right position.) Now apply pressure backward with your thigh on the bow handle and at the same time bend the bow by leaning forward from the waist and applying pressure with the right hand. The string loop held in the left hand can then be slipped into place in the upper nock. Before releasing pressure, make sure the string loops are firmly seated in the bow nocks.

The most important point to remember when using this method, and one which is largely overlooked in most instruction manuals, is to slip the upper string loop into place by feel. The eyes should be on the string alignment over the lower recurve. If this is done and the string is kept in line with the center of the bow limbs, there is no danger of twisting the limbs. Many archers who use this method look only at the upper string loop, not realizing that the bow is being bent out of line and allowing the string to angle off the side of the lower recurve. This practice, if continued, will work a twist into the limb.

Some archers still use the older, but less safe, "push-pull" stringing technique. Most authorities agree, however, that this technique is dangerous.

Use of foot harness to prevent twisting of bow limb. Photo by Shakespeare. (Stedman Studio.)

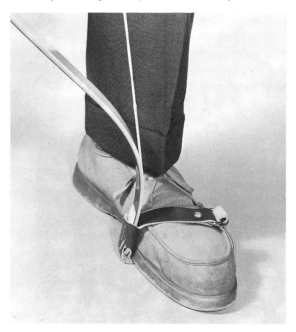

If the hand sliding the string loop up the bow limb should slip, as sometimes happens, the braced bow will recoil with tremendous force and the bow tip can easily put out an eye or break an eardrum. One may use this stringing and unstringing method for years without incident, yet one moment of carelessness can cause him to regret it. Play it safe. Use the step-across method, or better still, get a bowstringing device.

FISTMELE

Fistmele is an ancient English term for the distance between bow handle and string when the bow is braced. It was called "fist measure" because it was taken with the thumb extended from a clenched fist. A more modern term is "brace height."

On modern bows, brace height is measured at right angles to the string from the deepest cut in the handle on the face of the bow. Present-day bows come in such a variety of designs and sizes that it is impossible to state even a normal or average brace height except for straight-limbed bows. For these the distance should be about 6 inches. For all other bows, check the brace height recommended by the manufacturers in their catalogs.

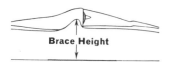

Brace Height

Nowadays, commercial bowstrings are precision made on machines, and the string supplied with a given bow model will usually give the right brace height within satisfactory limits.

The proper brace height for you depends upon your shooting style. There is no "exact" brace height which will give you maximum performance on various bows, or even on the same bow under varied conditions. New bowstrings will stretch but will settle to their final length if rubbed with a piece of cloth when the bow is braced. Brisk rubbing will heat the wax in the string and allow the strands to settle into their final position.

Keep the bowstring at the height which gives you the least noise or vibration while shooting, the least wrist slap, and straight flying arrows. Your brace height should never have to be low-

Use of bow square to determine proper fistmele and placement of nocking point.

ered, but to increase brace height the string is simply twisted a few turns in the direction that tightens the serving at the same time. (The "serving" is the bound portion of the string in the center and at both end loops.)

THE NOCKING POINT

After the bow has been braced, the next preliminary step is to establish and mark a nocking point, i.e., a point on the bowstring at an angle from the arrow rest slightly above the perpendicular—from ⅛ inch to 3/16 inch. The point itself consists either of several turns of thread or floss fastened with a whip finish and coated with clear fingernail polish or Duco-type cement, or one of the commercial slip-on or shrunk-on types available.

The nocking-point indicator is usually positioned so that when the arrow is properly placed on the string, its nock is snug up against the nocking-point indicator from below. A double nocking point, so that the arrow nock lies between them, is used by some archers. Seeing the arrow angled slightly downward from string to arrow rest may seem odd at first, but this position is more conducive to smooth getaway and flight than one in which the arrow is placed at right angles to the string and arrow rest.

The bow square, usually of aluminum or plastic, looks much like a T-square. With the bar of the T clipped to the bowstring and the arm resting on the arrow rest, the position for the nocking-point indicator can be quickly determined.

THE MASTER EYE

Many beginners start off using correctly matched equipment and proper form, yet wonder why their arrows don't hit the center of the target. For some of these people, the cause can be traced directly to an improper sight picture.

Anyone who is right-handed, yet whose left eye is the dominant eye, may miss the target consistently simply because he won't be shooting where he is looking.

Unless you use a bowsight, it is best to shoot with both eyes open. Your depth perception is greater, and in hunting, the field of vision is broader. However, if your master eye is not aligned with the arrow shaft the advantage is often lost.

The master eye is simply the stronger eye. You can find out in a few seconds which one this is for you. Extend your right arm and, with both eyes open, point your index finger at some object across the room. Now close your left eye. If the object is still in line with your pointing finger, your right eye is the master. If the object is out of line when the left eye is closed, try opening that eye and closing the right one. If the alignment is now correct, your left eye is the dominant one.

A nocking point on the bowstring insures correct placement of each arrow. (Stedman Studio.)

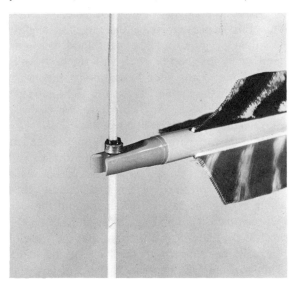

This means that if you are right-handed and your right eye is the master, things will proceed normally. But if you are right-handed with a stronger left eye, you might have to shoot the bow left-handed in order to take advantage of correct alignment. Many people have improved their shooting greatly after realizing this fact and have adjusted their shooting style accordingly.

Though proper use of the master eye will significantly improve the shooting of most people, there are exceptions. Some archers can shoot very well either right- or left-handed.

PROPER STEPS IN SHOOTING

Mothers in the Balearic Islands, near the coast of Spain, at one time used to hang their children's food on tree limbs, where it would stay until the youngsters could bring it down with bow and arrow. This rugged system made skilled marksmen of the children. For today's aspiring archers, however, the training technique of the Balearic people, though perhaps effective, is not practical.

It is entirely possible to learn the fundamentals of archery by reading good instructional material and then putting it into practice. Whenever possible, though, seek out competent coaching help. Errors in form or method often cannot be detected by self-examination. It takes the practiced eye of experience to spot them and show you how best to overcome them.

There are six steps in correct shooting technique: Standing, Nocking, Drawing, Holding and Aiming, Releasing and Follow-through.

The stance for most shooters should be at right angles to the target. Some tournament archers vary this stance by facing the target at slightly less than a right angle. The feet should be spread moderately for good balance, with the body erect but relaxed. Turn your head toward the target (over the left shoulder if you are right-handed) and don't move it. Any up, down, or sidewise movement of the head will affect your shot.

Hold the bow firmly, but not tightly, in the left hand (if you are right-handed). The thumb and forefinger should form a "V" at the inside of the handle. The pressure of the bow handle must come against the base of the thumb and the web between the thumb and forefinger and not on the heel of the palm. It is important that the back of the wrist be in line with the back of the hand. The wrist must not be bent, as that will put your forearm in a position where the string will strike it.

Holding the bow horizontally in front of you with the left hand, grasp an arrow by the nock between the thumb and forefinger of the right hand, lay it across the arrow rest with the cock feather up, and slide it back so the nock engages the bowstring just under the nocking point. Hook the first three fingers of your right hand, protected by the shooting glove, around the string, with the arrow nock between the first and second fingers. The string should lie along the crease of the first joint of the fingers. Then turn the bow to a vertical position.

Now you are ready to draw the bow. This is one continuous, uninterrupted action and consists of pushing the bow hand forward while at the same time the right hand draws the string and arrow back to the side of the face. The right arm should be held up on a level with the shoulder as it is drawn back so that the arm is in line with the arrow when at full draw. The shoulder muscles do most of the work of drawing. Do not grip the bow tightly, and make sure you take a full draw for uniform power.

Almost all beginners have trouble with arrows that fall off the rest as they are drawn back. This is caused by hooking the fingers more deeply as the bow is drawn. The increasing pressure against the arrow twists it away from the bow and off the rest.

The remedy is to reverse the action; in other words, crook the fingers more at the beginning

Supervised instruction starts the youngsters out right.

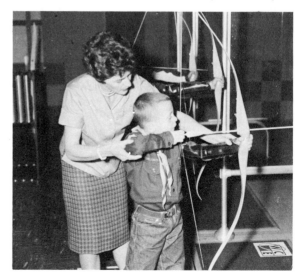

A properly outfitted teen-ager ready to enjoy the thrills of shooting. (Browning Arms Company Photo.)

Proper stance in relation to the target.

Correct method of placing the arrow on the bow-string.

Proper finger position on the bowstring.

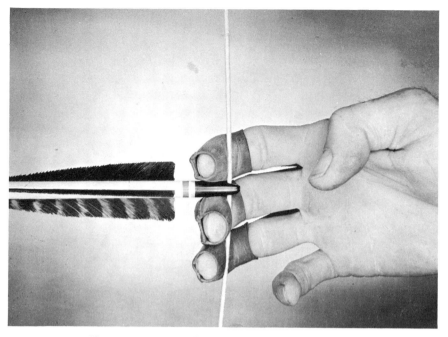

Close-up of proper finger position on the bowstring.

Correct draw. Head erect and drawing arm in alignment with the arrow.

Incorrect draw. Head is cocked forward and elbow of drawing arm is too low.

Correct position of drawing hand.

and let them straighten out as the pressure of the draw increases. This problem normally occurs only while learning and will disappear after the archer has done some practice shooting.

The draw is continued up to the "anchor point," a definite spot on the face to which either the index finger or middle finger of the drawing hand is brought on every draw. You should pick a spot that feels natural and comfortable for you and stick with it consistently. This is one of the most important points for uniform shooting results. You must draw to the same anchor point regardless of the distance to be shot. If this is not done, the shots will have varying degrees of power imparted to them, and consistent shooting will be impossible. Instinctive archers use the corner of the mouth as an anchor point, while sight shooters usually anchor at the bottom center of the chin.

When full draw is reached, there should be a slight pause, or holding period, during which the aiming is done. Although your arrow will be seen out of focus in the fringe of your vision, do not look directly at it. Concentrate on the very center of the target, letting the bow arm adjust instinctively for the range. This is the same aiming tech-

Instinctive anchor point.

Incorrect position of drawing hand. Back of hand is not straight and fingers are curled too far around the string.

nique as that used by bowlers, tennis players, and fast-draw enthusiasts (see aiming instructions in the following chapter). It is called "instinctive" aiming. You will be surprised how soon the bow arm automatically gives you the proper elevation for varying distances.

When holding the bow at full draw, it is necessary to continue to increase the pull by a tightening of the back muscles. While it may seem that one could just hold the bow at full draw, it can only be done by increasing the pull. It is like lifting and holding a heavy weight. It seems heavier the longer it is held, and it is necessary to continually lift harder to keep the weight at the same position.

So it is when holding a bow at full draw. If additional power is not applied the arrow will creep forward and you will not be at full draw for the release. Increasing the pull will automatically give you the correct release. When the release is made with the full power of the back muscles, the motion of the release hand can only be straight back, and that is the way it should be. The motion of the release hand out from the face rather

than straight back is faulty form that can only be corrected by tightening the back muscles during the hold. One does not really let go of the bowstring; it is rather like an escape of the string by means of this additional tension.

Follow-through on every shot is as important in archery as it is in golf, tennis, skeet, bowling, or horseshoes. Follow-through in archery means holding the bow arm perfectly still while the arrow is on its way to the target. Improper follow-through generally stems from the archer's anxiety to see where the arrow hits. If the follow-through is perfect, the bow hand will not drop at all and the bow will remain at the release position until the arrow strikes the target.

Archery success is achieved by developing a definite technique and this can best be done by enlisting the aid of an experienced archery instructor. It can also be done on your own by schooling yourself in the step-by-step fundamentals as outlined here. If you begin right, you will not have the problem of breaking bad habits later.

View showing proper arm alignment at full draw.

Correct follow-through. The hand should not be jerked away from the face when the release is made.

Chapter III

AIMING METHOD VARIATIONS

INSTINCTIVE SHOOTING

There are two principal systems of directing arrows to the target, and two variations which fall between them. The method used by the majority of archers is "instinctive" aiming, which was mentioned in the preceding chapter.

The term "instinctive shooting" more or less explains itself. It involves natural coordination between eyes and bow arm, with the eyes judging the distance to the target and the bow arm elevating the arrow to the correct height for that particular distance. This is the same aiming technique used in many other sports. If you are playing tennis you do not look at your racquet, but concentrate on where you want the ball to hit. If you are bowling you do not watch the ball, but concentrate instead on the pins, letting the arm send the ball where the eyes direct. The same technique applies to throwing a ball and shooting a slingshot.

Instinctive shooting requires the eyes to be focused only on the very center of the target. When concentrating on this spot, you also see the bow hand and part of the bow and arrow, but not clearly, for when your eyes are focused at a distance, objects close by will be out of focus or slightly blurred. However, you will find that even a blurred view of the arrow will give you a fair idea as to whether the elevation is proper and will serve as a good way to check yourself during the early stages of learning to shoot instinctively. As you progress with your practice you will slowly but surely begin to disregard the arrow almost entirely and concentrate more and more on

the center of the target. It is then you will discover that your bow arm is automatically taking care of the problem of elevation. An instinctive archer can do a good job of shooting when the target is only faintly illuminated and he is in complete darkness.

The truly instinctive archer will shoot from a somewhat less than upright position in contrast to the erect stance of the gap or sight shooter. Bending slightly (from the waist) is necessary so that the eye is directly above the arrow. This is vertical alignment, and if the arrow does not go where it is pointed it may be necessary to build out on the side of the bow where the arrow passes.

In this position the whole upper body leans forward from the waist, and the bow is canted at a comfortable angle. The controlling factor that determines this angle is the position of the eye directly above the arrow.

Intense concentration on the very center of whatever you are shooting at is the secret of instinctive shooting. This concentration must be overwhelming. The whole body from the toes to the top of the head must be involved in every shot. All other thinking must be erased from your mind. The very center of the target is the focus of your complete and undivided attention. The feet are spread apart somewhat. The knees are slightly bent in a semicrouched position as if you were about to spring on something. Concentration is the secret. The whole body is directed to this end as if you were funneling all your efforts to the pinpoint spot on the target. *Not the whole tar-*

Instinctive shooting from the crouching position.
Instinctive shooting requires a simultaneous push-and-pull action; in tournament or tar-get archery the bow arm is usually fully extended and the drawing done with the other.

get—just the center of it, whether it be a leaf, a deer, or an elephant.

Instinctive shooting is recommended for hunting and recreation only. The human body cannot stand up under the intense concentration necessary for tournament shooting: You would burn yourself out halfway through a contest. But no other method will provide the consistency of accuracy for hunting that instinctive shooting does. The instinctive method of drawing the arrow is the push-and-pull system. The bow hand is pushing the bow at the same time the other hand is drawing the arrow back. In other forms of aiming, the bow arm is usually fully extended, and the drawing is done with the other.

When first learning to shoot the bow, it is best to stand fairly close to the target—say, about 20 feet. This will insure more hits and fewer lost arrows. While learning, you should be interested more in correctly executing the proper shooting steps than in hitting the bull's-eye on every shot. Once you master the right technique, accuracy will follow. After you practice a few times at 20 feet, you will get the "feel" of how to aim at that particular distance. When you are hitting the target regularly at 20 feet, you can move back to 30 feet, then to 40 feet, and so on. At each distance you will find that the eyes and bow arm adjust very rapidly to the required change.

When ready to try shooting at longer distances, the aiming problem is complicated somewhat by arrow trajectory. The longer the shot the greater curve the arrow will take in flight. You must visualize this arc of the arrow in order to hit the target at varying distances. This again is part of the instinctive process and not nearly so complicated as it sounds. The more you practice and become used to your bow's performance, the better your range-finding ability will become and the more regularly you will hit targets even a considerable distance away. Distance to the target is not considered in terms of yards. Experience will teach a "feel" for the range, and your bow hand will provide the correct elevation instantly.

There are two reasons for the continued popularity of instinctive shooting. First is the thrill of achieving accuracy with nothing but the abilities nature gave you, with no dependence upon mechanical aids. Second, instinctive shooting is ideally suited to bowhunting when split-second decisions have to be made and shots taken rapidly

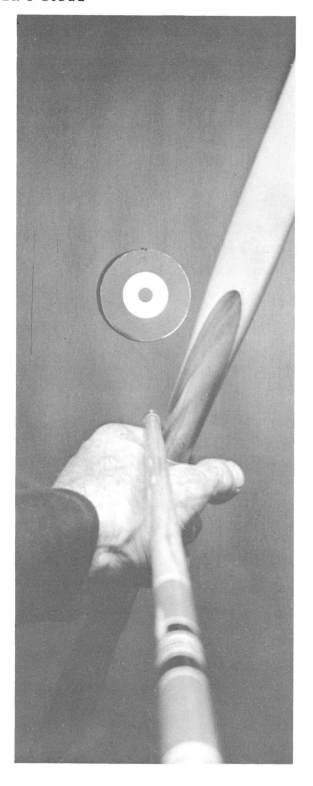

Instinctive shooter's view.

Instinctive shooting from a standing position. (Porton & Peel.)

limbs. Such flexibility of technique is a distinct hunting advantage. So, for the archer interested mainly in bowhunting, and in roving or field-range shooting in preparation for hunting, the instinctive style of aiming is the best.

GAP SHOOTING

Another type of sighting, akin to the instinctive method, is called "gap shooting." In this method the archer makes use of a "space picture," i.e., he looks at the target and nothing else but is still conscious of seeing the amount of space between the arrow tip and the target. The size of this space or gap becomes a measure of the angle of elevation, and the archer either consciously or unconsciously uses this measure for a distance check.

There is a certain distance when the tip of the arrow will be sighted right on the target. This will be known as *your* point-blank range. Beyond this range the point of the arrow must be sighted higher. This method involves some trial and error until you are able to pick the right aiming gap, or space picture, for any given distance.

Fingers positioned immediately below normal nocking point for a medium range shot. For a longer range shot, the forefinger might be placed above the arrow nock.

THREE FINGERS UNDER

This method is characterized by putting all three drawing fingers underneath the arrow instead of holding the arrow nock between the first and second fingers. The arrow nock must

and from awkward positions. Instinctive shooters can loose an arrow accurately toward a target quicker than sight shooters. Also, the instinctive hunter is not hampered with a set body position but can, and often does, shoot from unusual positions such as crouching, kneeling or even sitting. He can also cant the bow to one side in order to shoot from heavy brush or under low-hanging

fit the bowstring firmly to hold it in place without assistance during the draw. An advantage of this style is that the archer can get the arrow closer to the eye with a normal anchor position. Many archers using this style move the anchor point up from the corner of the mouth to the cheekbone for close shooting. This is much like looking down a gun barrel. It is easier to aim because the angle of the arrow in relation to the eye is less acute.

STRING WALKING

This is a variation of the three-fingers-under

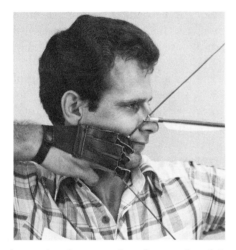

Anchor point the same, but fingers placed lower on the string thus bringing the nocking point higher. This allows sighting directly down the arrow for close range shooting.

method. But instead of changing the anchor point contact from the first to the second or third finger tip, the regular anchor contact is kept (normally at the corner of the mouth) and the three drawing fingers move farther down the bowstring. The lower the fingers are on the string, the closer the arrow is to the eye. For very close range shooting of 10 to 20 yards the arrow can be immediately below the eye and the gun barrel effect is most accurate, the arrow flying with an arc nearly the same as the line of sight. Through various finger placements the archer can establish a sight picture that is always the same and still allow for the arrow arriving at the bull's-eye. The general rule is that the farther the nock is from the eye, the farther the arrow will travel. Additional serving points in white or various colors are added to the bowstring and used to mark the correct finger

positions for the various yardages being shot. It is a very effective method that enables the target archer or bowhunter who masters it to shoot almost as accurately as one using a bow sight.

SNAP SHOOTING

Snap shooting, closely allied with "freezing" (see page 48), is an affliction affecting the coordination between eye and muscle that makes it impossible to reach full draw before releasing the arrow. There are two causes: a bow that is too

Eye should be directly above the arrow; this placing determines the angle of the bow. (William C. Clifton.)

In shooting with the aid of a bowsight it is customary to lower the anchor point from the side of the face to just under the center of the chin.

At full draw in bowsight shooting, the bowstring is aligned with the center of the chin and tip of the nose.

View of target bull's-eye through a bowsight.

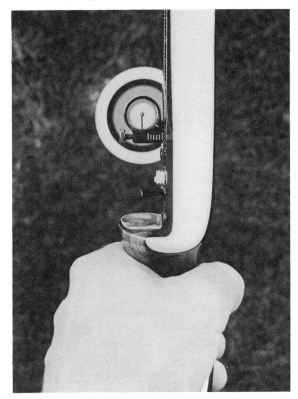

heavy in draw weight, and shooting too quickly. Shooting too quickly is triggered by the overwhelming desire to see your arrow in the bull's-eye of the target. Not drawing fully to anchor, or releasing before the anchor point is reached, are the symptoms.

In condemning snap shooting, it must be pointed out that this fault comes in two varieties. The short draw, in which the release is made before getting back to the anchor point, must be avoided at all costs. Consistent accuracy can never be attained either on the target range or in the hunting field so long as this fault is present. On the other hand, the truly instinctive shooter can also be a snap shooter. The difference between the short-draw shooter and the truly instinctive snap shooter—and there is a great difference—is that the latter always comes to full draw at the anchor point, even though there is little or no pause before release. The so-called instinctive aiming is done during the push-and-pull motions of the draw, and after some practice, one is "on target" when full draw is reached and the arrow is released.

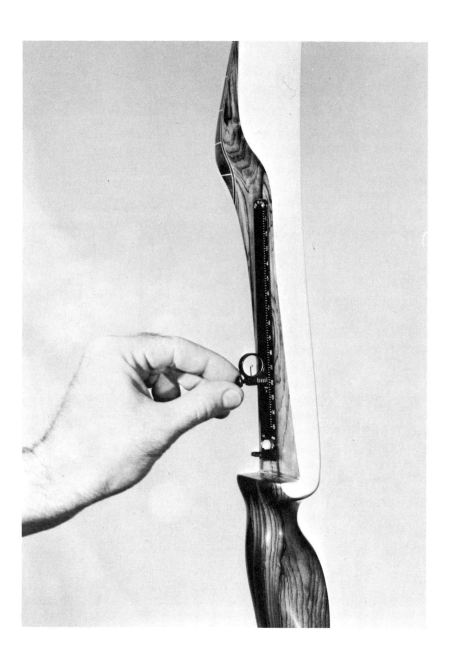

Bowsight built into a bow with adjustments for elevation and windage.

SHOOTING WITH A SIGHT

Although I personally do not use a bowsight, since I learned to shoot the bow before sights came into use, it is my belief that learning to shoot with a bowsight is the best way, even though one may be interested in hunting only. Shooting with a sight will reveal bad form more quickly than shooting without it.

Despite the fact that sights are relatively new in archery, their use is now universal. "Free-stylers" (the term for archers who use a mechanical aiming device on their bows) have won every major tournament in all types of competition, and increasing numbers of bowhunters are becoming converts to the use of a sight each year. In recent years thousands of men, women and children have been introduced to archery in indoor archery lanes. Without exception, instructors in such establishments have found that the fastest way to help beginners achieve accuracy is by starting them out with a bowsight.

There are a great many makes of bowsights on the market. These range from a single fixed or movable pin to a set of precision optics. The majority of sights employ an adjustable post, pin, prism, or cross-hairs protruding from the side of the bow, which can be moved up or down on a fixed bar, permitting the archer to sight directly on the target from any distance. A white tape is usually attached to the fixed sight bar, on which the archer marks his distance settings as the bow is sighted in. Elevation is changed by sliding the sight up or down on the bar. Horizontal correction can also be made by adjusting the pin or aperture to increase or decrease the distance it projects beyond the side of the bow.

The archer has to shoot a number of arrows at each distance to determine just where the sight should be set for that distance, and then mark the graduation on the sight bar. In adjusting for elevation, the sight should be moved up to lower the striking point of the arrow, and lowered to raise it. In other words, the farther you are shooting the lower your sight will be. Once the distance settings have been determined and marked on the bar, you can shoot at any known distance simply by moving the sight setting to that mark.

A few of today's finer tournament bows have the bowsight built into the bow as an integral part; some of these bows come equipped with a system of interchangeable accessories such as fluorescent posts, prisms, and rings with cross-hairs. Special telescopic sights are also being produced by well-known optical firms for use on bows.

In shooting with the aid of a bowsight it is customary to lower the anchor point from the side of the face to just under the center of the chin. At full draw the bowstring is aligned with the center of the chin and tip of the nose. In order to achieve the correct sighting picture, the free-styler must hold his bow in a straight up-and-down position. It is possible when using a sight for hunting to use a high side of the face anchor, but the bow should not be canted.

Once proper shooting form has been established, the archer interested in bowhunting can then make the switch to instinctive shooting if desired. Many instinctive shooters who develop poor holding or releasing habits often turn to the temporary use of a bowsight to correct the problems.

POINT-OF-AIM

In years gone by, most beginners in archery were taught the point-of-aim method right from the start. The point-of-aim shooter does not look at the target. He aims over the tip of the arrow at a predetermined spot or marker placed on the ground between the shooter and the target. He never shifts his eyes to the target face until after the release. As can be seen, this method involves quite a bit of trial and error until one is able to pick the right aiming spot for any given distance.

Today this method has been largely replaced by the use of bowsights.

There are constant arguments as to the respective merits of the various sighting systems. Suffice it to say that each has its place. The prospective archer should try them all, decide which is best for his particular style and type of shooting, and stick with it, yet at the same time be tolerant of those who use another system.

Chapter IV

COMMON SHOOTING FAULTS AND HOW TO CORRECT THEM

Having outfitted yourself with a bow of the right draw weight and properly matching arrows, and having mastered the fundamental steps of good shooting, you are well on the way to becoming a skilled archer. Before you can make real progress, however, you must correct small errors as they occur.

Everyone who shoots the bow will face these problems. The best equipment in the world won't overcome them, and if not checked promptly before becoming habitual, they may not be easy to correct. It is usually very difficult for a beginner to detect his own mistakes, and this is where a qualified instructor comes in handy. Lacking an instructor, a novice can help evaluate his errors by temporary use of a bowsight. If you do not wish to use a bowsight for hunting or field shooting, it is still advisable to try one out while learning. The good holding and releasing habits it develops will carry over to instinctive shooting.

As you progress in shooting, your arrows will start to group closely together in the target. However, while your arrows may be grouped, the grouping may be high, low, or to one side of the target's center. This of course is better than having one arrow in the center and the rest scattered. A group at least shows consistency in shooting technique. The following suggestions may help move the arrow group closer to where it should be.

Arrows Grouping Too High

You may be opening your mouth as you shoot, thus lowering your anchor point. You may also be slightly overdrawing by pulling the bowstring back beyond your regular anchor point. Also, your nocking point may have slipped down slightly.

Arrows Grouping Too Low

Either you are not drawing fully to your anchor point, or you are allowing the string hand to creep forward at the instant of shooting.

Arrows Grouping to the Right

Caused either by arrows of insufficient spine for the bow weight, or by holding the bowstring farther in than normally on the drawing fingers. Also, you may not be aligning your body at right angles to the target, thus changing the angle of draw.

Arrows Grouping to the Left

Caused either by arrows of the wrong spine, or by moving the string hand away from the anchor point. Too tight a grip on the bow is another cause. The bow must always "float" between the thumb and knuckle.

Arrows Grouping Both High and to the Right

Can be caused by jerking or plucking the drawing hand back and inward as the arrow is

This archer displays good follow-through. Release hand has not moved away from his face, and bow arm will not move until the arrow strikes the target. (B. Pearson Photo.)

Correct position of bow hand. Pressure of the bow hand is against the base of the thumb and web between thumb and first finger.

Incorrect position of bow hand. Wrist not straight and bow being heeled against palm of hand.

View of correct wrist position of bow hand. Arm, wrist, and hand are in alignment with pressure of bow against base of thumb.

View of incorrect position of wrist. Hand cocked too far in on bow handle. This will cause erratic arrow flight, bowstring slapping the arm, and a tired bow arm.

released. Another cause is holding the bowstring farther in than normally on the drawing fingers.

Arrows Grouping Both Left and Low

Caused by dropping the bow arm as the arrow is released. You must follow through by holding your position until the arrow hits the target.

OTHER ERRORS

If you have trouble with arrows "porpoising," or flying erratically, and you know they are spined correctly for your bow, the trouble may be a nocking point that is too low. Try moving it up $\frac{1}{16}$ to $\frac{1}{8}$ inch.

Arrows that drift to one side on long shots can be caused by turning the bow hand too far in-

ward. Grasping the bow so that the wrist is in straight alignment with the arm is a cure for this.

One fairly common cause of erratic arrow flight or arrows drifting too far to either right or left is often hard to detect by the shooter. The source of this problem lies in the arrow plate. The arrow plate is a piece of leather, plastic, or metal on the side of the bow against which the arrow shaft rides when placed on the arrow rest. Its purpose is to prevent marking the bow wood through continual contact with arrows. Due to variances in individual shooting style, the arrow plate originally supplied on a bow, while right for the majority of archers, may not give satisfactory results for everyone. A few of today's bow models have adjustable arrow plates which can be moved in or out until set just right for the shooter's style. Bows without an adjustable arrow plate can still be "tuned" to the individual by building up the plate with additional layers of leather or other suitable material. These spacers can be taped on for trial shooting and later glued on. As an example, I find that for my own shooting style it is necessary to build up my arrow plates a full ¼ inch.

Arrows that slap the bow can be caused by gripping the bow too tightly. This can be corrected by relaxing the grip a bit. If the fistmele is too low, the back of the arrow may slap the bow as it passes. Try a few twists in the bowstring to raise the brace height. Also, the nocking point may be too low.

A bowstring that slaps the bow arm can be caused either by turning the wrist of the bow hand too far in on the bow or by letting the elbow of the bow arm rotate too far inward. Another, more obvious cause would be jerking on the release. Also, check to make sure the back of your wrist is in line with your arm.

You cannot vary your anchor point and expect consistent results. Raising, lowering or tilting the head will displace the anchor point and cause erratic arrow flight. Developing a consistently uniform stance is the answer.

Uneven tension of the fingers on the bowstring is a common cause of poor releases. If one or two fingers are carrying most of the draw load, the lazy one will drag on release. Keep the wrist of your drawing hand straight but relaxed and let all three drawing fingers share equally in the load.

THE PROBLEM OF FREEZING

Of all the maladies that plague archers, oldtimers as well as beginners, "freezing" is the most virulent and the hardest to overcome. Freezing is the inability to move the aim or sight to the center of the target and hold it there while executing a correct release. It is difficult to believe that this condition can exist unless one has experienced it. The shooter is seized by a condition likened to buck fever. A top tournament shooter can become a snap shooter and drop to the lower ranks. What happens is that the eye triggers the release before the mind can control it.

The only known cure to correct freezing, or snap shooting due to overanxiety, involves a device called a "clicker." This is a light strip of springy metal mounted in the sight window of the bow just in front of the arrow rest, so that it is positioned at the end of the arrow point at full draw. The arrow is drawn between the bow surface and the clicker. When normal draw is reached, steady aim is taken, and then the draw is slightly increased by moving the drawing hand. This brings the arrow point clear of the clicker, and the sound of the metal strip against the sight window automatically triggers your reflexes to release the arrow. When using a clicker, be deliberate and follow through with aiming and drawing tension so that your release is smooth and dynamic. To develop even greater control, practice holding your release from one half to a full second or more after the "click" has occurred. Use of this device has restored self-confidence and positive control to many archers.

Do not let this chapter on shooting faults dis-

A bow sling is useful for the archer with a loose bow grip, as it insures against the bow being dropped upon release of the arrow.

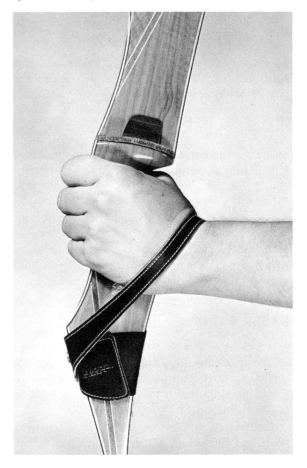

courage you. Some of the faults listed herein may occur, but certainly not all of them, and most are easy to correct. Remember that archery is a game of skill, and skill in any endeavor is acquired only by practice and proper technique. A bow used correctly is an accurate instrument, and its effectiveness is limited only by the development of the individual archer.

The clicker is a useful gadget to correct the problem of preliminary release. (Stedman Studio.)

Chapter V

RECREATIONAL ARCHERY

Archery is essentially a sport of individual accomplishment. Whatever degree of skill you attain is due mainly to your own efforts. Although archers usually shoot in groups, the sport is so adaptable that you can spend many pleasant hours shooting by yourself. It can be enjoyed the year round, indoors and out, and at any period in your life from early youth to advanced age.

Archery is a natural "togetherness" sport. To many couples who find satisfaction in spending leisure hours together, archery provides opportunities unequaled in most other sports. Almost every family unit welcomes a form of healthful recreation that involves all its members. Husband and wife become real shooting partners. And watch out for the youngsters! They may, and usually do, end up by becoming more expert than the adults. Parents can take pride not only in sharing a recreational interest with their children but in watching their growing skill as well.

Archery can be practiced in your own backyard, and in fact a multicolored target makes an attractive lawn decoration. Target butts of banded hay or excelsior can be bought cheaply and give good service. The butt should be placed in a position so that the areas behind and to the sides will not be danger spots if your arrows miss. Rising ground behind the butt or the side of a garage or shed will keep high arrows from taking off. Two additional bales of hay a few feet behind the target butt also make a good backstop. Target faces are attached to the butt with large pins which can be made from wire coat hangers. With such a setup, members of the family can learn and practice in whatever free time is available. A

word of caution here: When youngsters are in the learning stage, do not turn them loose on their own. Proper supervision will keep your neighbors peaceful.

ARCHERY CLUBS

The way to get the most fun out of archery is to join a club, of which there are many thousands all over the country. Some are target clubs shooting under the rules of the National Archery Association, and others are field archery clubs affiliated with the National Field Archery Association. In addition, there are many independent groups who exchange shoots with other clubs in their immediate area.

Later in this book the differences and similarities among these various groups are explored. For now it is enough to know that wherever you live, the chances are good that there is an archery club of some kind close by. As an example, there are within a radius of 40 miles of the heart of New York City more than 150 archery clubs that either own or have access to shooting ranges. If you have never heard of a club in your area, check with the Chamber of Commerce and with local sporting goods dealers who stock archery equipment. If they cannot help you, contact the N.A.A. or the N.F.A.A. to find the nearest affiliated club or league. And in the rare event there aren't any clubs close by, you might consider starting one. It isn't hard, and instructions on how to go about it will be found in Chapter VII.

Membership in an archery club has two big ad-

A family group enjoying the recreation of backyard archery practice.

vantages. First and foremost is having a place to shoot, either in fun or in competition, with others who enjoy the same sport. Second is the opportunity a club offers to the inexperienced archer to gain the advice of more experienced members on shooting form, special tackle, etc.

ROVING

In addition to backyard fun and participation in club activities, there are other forms of archery that can be enjoyed for relaxation and exercise. One excellent variation, which can be played by two or more archers, is called "roving." Roving is actually a holdover from the days when the bow and arrow was the principal weapon of warfare in England. At that time roving courses were es-

tablished between towns by royal edict to keep the young men in good shooting form.

All that is needed is a tract of land such as a woodlot, meadow, pasture, or field. Farmlands are ideally suited to roving. The game is started by one archer who picks a suitable mark such as a tuft of grass, a scrap of paper, a small mound, etc. All archers present shoot in turn at the mark picked, and the one who comes closest or who gets the best hit has the privilege of picking a mark for the next shot. The game can be spiced up a bit by keeping score. Needless to say, this is instinctive shooting at its best, and the participants quickly become good judges of distance over varying terrain. This is particularly fine practice for the archer who intends to do some

Man and wife scoring a practice round. (Browning Arms Company Photo.)

bowhunting. After a season of this kind of shooting, the bowman is well prepared for shots at game within reasonable range.

ARCHERY GOLF

Archery golf is great fun and lends itself ideally to family participation. As the name implies, it is similar to golf except that bows and arrows are used in place of clubs and golf balls. The ideal setup is to have access to a regular golf course. Naturally, archery golf cannot be played while regular golfers are on the course. Sometimes, however, archers can make arrangements with a local golf club to use the course on days when no golfers are present or perhaps in early morning hours before the regular golfers show up or during the winter months.

A regulation golf course is by no means a necessity for this sport. Often it is best to hunt up a tract of vacant ground (rolling farmlands are ideal) and obtain permission from the owner for its use. All you need to lay out a course are some stakes topped with a cloth flag, for marking shooting positions and target locations. In laying out your own course, you can work considerable variation into the distances from "tee" to "hole"

—say, from 50 yards to 400 yards or more, depending largely on how much space is available. Whenever possible, locate the "holes" on mounds or banks where a miss means a long return shot. If playing on a regular golf course, it is a good idea to place the target positions just off the green, on top of a bunker or sand trap. The "hole" or target is any soft ball such as a tennis ball. When archers approach the green and get ready to "putt," the ball is placed on a wire stand about 2 feet above the ground. Each group should carry its own stand and ball. While no special archery equipment is needed to play, some variation of arrows is helpful. A lightweight arrow with small fletching will give more distance on "drives." Field points on approach arrows will keep them from skidding. Arrows with flu-flu fletching are handy for close shots, and "putters" should have blunt points.

Scoring is the same as in regular golf, i.e., number of strokes taken on each hole. No other rules are necessary, but there are a few helpful regulations as recommended by the N.F.A.A.: (1) No preliminary practice allowed on the course. (2) All archers in a group shoot one arrow from tee toward target. (3) In each succeeding shot the man whose arrow is farthest from the target shoots first. (4) To "hole out," the ball must be knocked from its stand. (5) In case of a lost arrow, one point must be added to the contestant's score and the next shot made from a point as near as possible to where the arrow was lost. (6) In case of a tie, those involved shall continue shooting until the tie is broken.

INDOOR LANES

In many areas of the country, installation of commercial indoor archery ranges has placed archery on a par with bowling and other indoor sports. Shooting lanes in such installations are about the size and length of bowling alleys, with space for spectators behind the shooting lines. At each shooting position is a console for controlling the target location and for scoring. After shooting a round of arrows, the archer pushes a button on the console and the target moves quietly and quickly to the shooting line. The contestant adds up his score and withdraws his arrows. He then selects a control button to return the target to the desired shooting position

for another round. Dividers and other built-in safety features are standard equipment in each lane.

A high percentage of participants are newcomers to the sport and so do not have their own equipment. Therefore, the ranges set up a rental service which stocks bows of various draw weights, target arrows, arm guards, and shooting gloves. Once the novice learns how to shoot, he or she can purchase a variety of equipment in the range pro shop. Usually the range provides initial instruction without cost, and advanced instruction at a very nominal fee. League play is available for those past the learning stage, and charges are similar to bowling fees. A variety of archery games are also available for families or other interested groups to play at any time. Because instinctive archers and those using bowsights are often intermingled in league shooting, handicap systems in scoring are popular. The average archer, after learning the fundamentals, can exercise any degree of the competitive impulse, or be a complete individualist if he so chooses by concentrating on improving his target skill.

Indoor archery lanes are beginning to spread throughout the country. (N.S.G.A. Photo. William Langley.)

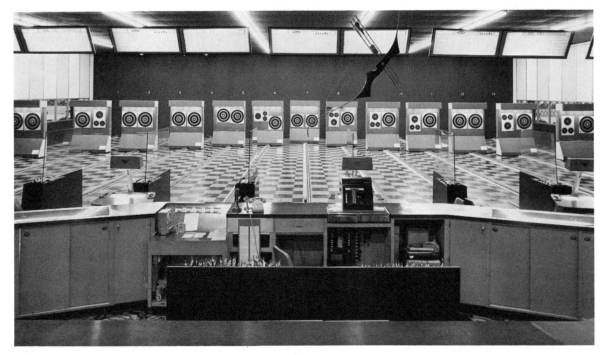

Archers shooting in indoor lanes. (N.S.G.A. Photo. Al Pottorf.)

View of indoor lanes from behind the shooting positions, showing the table consoles for moving the targets and scoring.

Competitive indoor money tournaments such as this one in Las Vegas are growing in popularity. (Glenn Helgeland photo.)

Chapter VI

TARGET ARCHERY

Competitive archery today has two major divisions: target and field. Usually an archer is involved in either one or the other, although a growing number enjoy both phases of the sport.

Target archery is the oldest competitive sport among American bowmen, who copied it from the classic form dominant in England and the western European countries. The first American target-archery group on record was the United Bowmen of Philadelphia, founded in 1828. Thirty-some years later the onset of the Civil War put an end to such frivolous sport. However, about twenty years later the archery exploits and writings of Maurice and Will Thompson brought on a resurgence of interest, and in 1879 Maurice was instrumental in creating the National Archery Association. This organization has lasted since that time and is thriving today. In 1881, women began to shoot the English Double National Round, and in 1882 the division of Flight Shooting was introduced. The American Round was invented in 1883 for those who did not care for shooting over the 100-yard range of the standard York Round. In addition, there are several other rounds considered standard in championship tournaments.

Target courses are laid out over level terrain and, when possible, so that shooting is from south to north. Target butts are spaced evenly from 4 to 6 yards apart. At least every third target has a small colored flag projecting 2 or 3 feet above it to serve as a wind indicator. Shooting positions are laid out along straight lines parallel to and at carefully measured distances from the targets. Four archers, shooting two at a time at the same target, is the customary assignment. The faces themselves are 48 inches in diameter with a center gold spot, or bull's-eye, some 9.6 inches in diameter, surrounded by four concentric bands of red, blue, black and white.

Any type of hand-held bow, except compounds, is allowed in target archery, and any kind of sight, point-of-aim or other variety of aiming device, may be used. Participants are classed in the following groups:

Men	18 years or over
Women	18 years or over
Intermediate Boys	15 to 18
Intermediate Girls	15 to 18
Junior Boys	12 to 15
Junior Girls	12 to 15
Cadet Boys	less than 12
Cadet Girls	less than 12

Arrows are shot in groups, or "ends," of six, after which the contestants, on a given signal, advance to the targets to score the results. Scoring values in the standard target face are: Gold—9, Red—7, Blue—5, Black—3, White—1. Thus, a perfect end of six arrows in the gold would score 54 points. Standard Championship Rounds consist of the following:

1—YORK ROUND (Men)
   72 arrows at 100 yards
   48 arrows at 80 yards
   24 arrows at 60 yards (Total: 144 arrows)

CLOUT SHOOTING

Clout shooting is another archery target game that originated in England. It differs from other shooting in that the target is laid out flat on the ground. The target face itself is in a ratio of 12 to 1 to a standard target face. In other words, the bull's-eye measures 9.6 feet across, and the outer target diameter is 48 feet. The center is marked by a white flag or colored disk on a wood stake. Usual distances shot are 180 yards for men and 140 yards for women.

A good system is to lay out two targets, one at each end of a field, so that, as in horseshoes, you can score both going and coming. A round consists of six arrows per archer. After all contestants have shot and approached the target, the arrows are pulled and laid in the ring in which they hit, ready for scoring. Scoring values are the same as on regulation target faces.

WAND SHOOTING

In the tales of Robin Hood we read of such feats as splitting a willow wand repeatedly at 150 yards. In the light of present knowledge of materials and technology, such shooting would have been either impossible or lucky in the extreme. Wand shooting today is done at a distance of 100 yards for men and 60 yards for women. The target is a strip of soft wood 2 inches wide and projecting 6 feet up from the ground. Thirty-six arrows constitute an end. Only those arrows actually imbedded in the wand, or witnessed rebounds, count as hits. This is a very useful round for perfecting a steady hold and clean release.

CROSSBOWS

The crossbow, which is released by a trigger, is classified as a mechanical device rather than as a regulation bow. Crossbowmen, therefore, do not compete with longbowmen but have a separate division within the N.A.A. and compete only against each other.

All crossbows used in N.A.A. tournaments must be drawn or cocked by hand with no aiding devices. No telescopic or magnifying sights are permitted. Rectangular bales are not considered suitable for crossbow use; target backstops are round bosses of woven or compressed marsh grass or straw, approximately 53 inches in diame-

Typical modern crossbows. (National Company of Crossbowmen Photo.)

Excellent crossbow form. The shooter is Col. Francis E. Pierce, Ret., who has held every national crossbow record, and who is First Captain of the National Company of Crossbowmen. (National Company of Crossbowmen.)

ter. The target face is one half the size of the faces used by longbowmen for the distance shot, but is similar in other respects except that the gold center may be white for better visibility. Exceptions occur in the Clout Round, where the same size target is used as in the longbow division, and in the King's Round, which has no counterpart in the longbow division.

Arrows for crossbows are called "bolts" or "darts" and may be made of any material and of varying lengths. They are considerably shorter than regular arrows, averaging between 8 and 15 inches in length.

Crossbowmen shoot from a standing position, and no rests are allowed for the bow or bow arm. Two crossbowmen per target is the normal assignment, and only one contestant shoots at a time, releasing one bolt and then stepping back from the shooting line after his turn.

The National Crossbow Championship for both men and women is determined by the highest total scores shot in the Quadruple American Round. Tournament officials may at their discretion add other events as they choose, such as the Clout Round, King's Round or novelty rounds, but the scores of these events do not count in determining the champions.

The King's Round is shot in national meets only by the crossbowmen making the highest individual American Round scores while participating in the Championship Quadruple American Round. Target face for the King's Round contest is a special 48-inch face containing six gold areas of 4¾-inch diameter, spaced on an 18-inch radius at 12-, 2-, 4-, 6-, and 8-o'clock positions respectively. Within each of the gold areas is a 1-inch black center bull's-eye. Distance shot is 40 yards.

Bolts must cut the gold to score, each hit in the gold counting nine points while a hit in the black spot counts ten. The contestant making the highest score is given the title of King (or Queen) and is awarded a special prize called the Steven's King's Round Dagger, which may be held by the recipient for the tournament year.

Crossbow events with their accompanying heraldry form a very colorful segment of the National Target Championship tourneys.

Chapter VII

FIELD ARCHERY

Target archery, with very few exceptions, was the only form of the sport practiced in America up to the twentieth century. In the early 1930s, however, a group of California bowhunters got together and decided that formalized target shooting over exact distances was not good bowhunting practice. They devised a type of course laid out in the woods under natural hunting conditions, with all targets placed at unknown and varying distances. All shooting was instinctive and mechanical aiming aids were not allowed. Their first range, built in 1934, was called a "field course"; consequently, when they organized on a national scale, in 1939, their organization was named the National Field Archery Association.

Field archery was originally planned to be more of a game than a competition; its objectives were to shoot for fun and to acquire shooting skill under conditions as close to hunting as possible. Courses were laid out in two fourteen-target units, in woods cover and uneven terrain, and with only narrow cleared lanes between shooting positions and targets.

In recent years, due largely to the organization's acceptance of free-style advocates, field archery has actually become another form of target archery. Courses are now often built in completely brushed-out woods or in open fields. Distances from shooting positions to targets are now measured and are usually marked on the shooting-position stakes. More and more people are seen on field courses who have no interest in bowhunting and no interest in instinctive shooting. To these people, field archery is a competitive version of target archery. For target archers, it is an excellent alternate sport because it offers more variety than do the N.A.A. ranges.

Standard field-archery targets are of various sizes, depending on the distance to be shot. They are 6, 12, 18, and 24 inches in diameter. There are only two scoring areas: a center white bull's-eye, which counts five, and an outer black ring, which counts three. The archer shoots four arrows at each target, and the perfect score per target is twenty. Targets are laid out at distances of from 15 feet to 80 yards, some having a different shooting position for each arrow.

In addition to the standard Field Round, tournaments usually include a Hunter's Round and an Animal Round. Hunter's Round targets are completely black except for a small white center spot; the line dividing the scoring values is invisible from the shooting position. Animal targets are colorful reproductions of game such as deer, bear, wild turkey and rabbits. The scoring area is divided into two parts. The higher-scoring part is an oblong covering the most vital parts, while the lower-scoring area is the space between the high-scoring area and the hair, skin or feather line of the represented animal. Originally this round was shot with broadhead arrows, but now regular target arrows are used.

In field-archery tournaments, shooters are divided into classes depending on age, sex and past scoring ability. And as in target archery, there are now major divisions based on shooting style, i.e., instinctive or free-style.

Field archery is a wonderful weekend togetherness sport.

Field-range targets are laid out with different shooting positions to better simulate hunting positions.

Uneven terrain makes for interesting shooting on the field course.

Archery is a sport for all ages, being one of the few active participant sports which can be enjoyed throughout a lifetime.

Field archery's classification system is as follows: The Instinctive Division with sixteen classes consisting of five for men, five for women, Intermediate Boys, Intermediate Girls, Junior Boys, Junior Girls, Cub Boys, and Cub Girls. The same number of classes exist in the Freestyle Division.

Presently the N.F.A.A. is a closely knit federation of state associations, each with its Field Governor. Each affiliated club must have its range inspected and approved by inspectors appointed by the Field Governor. Individually affiliated clubs may handle shooting divisions in their own way. Some clubs are still solely instinctive, some are mixed instinctive and free-style, and others are totally free-style.

ARCHERY CLUBS

The archery club with more than 100 active members is an exception. Usually a small group of archers interested in having their own organi-

zation and shooting area form a club. Original members bring in friends and relatives, interest them in the sport, and perhaps eventually obtain enough membership dues to buy or rent land for a range and erect a clubhouse or other facilities.

Some of these clubs are composed of target archers who shoot the fixed N.A.A. rounds. However, the clubs most prevalent today are made up of field archers. The roving type of shooting seems to be the most interesting for family groups and often offers the best training grounds for the prospective bowhunter. A club may be entirely independent or may associate with several other clubs in the area to form a league. They may affiliate with their state archery association and with the national organization of their choice.

There are quite a few possibilities for obtaining use of land for a range. If the club is interested in target archery, members can contact the local school-district office, the Y.M.C.A., Boy Scout camp, or municipal park authority. Often such organizations can be prevailed upon to provide range facilities on ground which is already maintained for recreational purposes. In fact, one or more of these may already have an archery program which could be expanded to cover your needs.

The club committee contacting such people should not be hesitant in presenting their needs and problems. More often than not, the persons interviewed will be as interested in the newfound sport as the archers, since a properly run club can help them do their job by providing another fine recreational program for the community.

With respect to field archery, one of the best places to inquire about land is at the State Conservation or Fish & Game Commission Headquarters. In many states, much of the wooded area between towns is public forest land. The possibility of leasing enough such land for a range is excellent, and the charges are very reasonable. Another good possibility is a local Sportsmen's Club or Rod & Gun Club. Such clubs often have extra space, and, as archery is rapidly gaining favor among outdoorsmen, they may well be receptive to adding another shooting variation.

Still a third possibility is to inquire of farmers who have woodlots or fallow land on their property. Deserted farms, too, are good bets. But in any event, locate the owner, get his permission for use, assure him his property will not be littered or otherwise damaged, and pay him a rental fee.

Good points for both existing and prospective archery clubs to keep in mind for successful operation and growth are these: (a) An eager, hard-working secretary is the most important officer your club can have. (b) Hold regular meetings at least once a month. (c) Weekly league shooting with two- or three-man teams using an 80 percent handicap basis to even out the chances for beginners and young members. (d) Novelty shoots are endless in variety, popular with everyone, and should be held often. (e) Don't neglect the juniors. Give them a voice in meetings and responsibility in helping care for the range. They are the future of any club. (f) The women members are perhaps the most important segment, keeping the club active by serving lunches at shoots, refreshments at meetings, refurbishing the club treasury through bake sales,

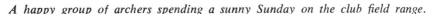

A happy group of archers spending a sunny Sunday on the club field range.

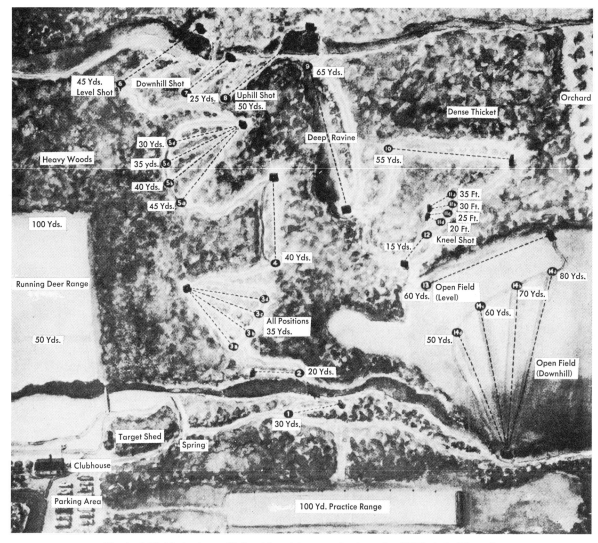

Typical Field Archery Club with a 14-target basic unit. (N.F.A.A. Photo.)

etc. (g) Don't let your group become "trophy happy." Never forget that archery at the club level should be mostly for fun. (h) Grassroots politicking pays off. Invite local game wardens, school physical-education instructors, archery dealers, range-land owners, etc., to the meetings. Show interest in them, and they'll be interested in you—and give you help when you need it.

FIELD RANGES

For laying out a 14-target field course, a tract of about 10 acres of land, and twice that for a 28-target range, will be needed. Assuming you have obtained the use of a suitable area, the first step is to pick a central spot for headquarters.

That is where the target layouts will start and end. Keep in mind space for a parking area, picnic or bonfire area, and a site for a future shelter or clubhouse. Don't be too hasty in laying out the course itself. Take advantage of uneven terrain for a variety of shooting positions, with targets both uphill and down. Basically, the trail connecting target positions should be circular so that shooters end up close to their starting point. A 28-target range can be laid out in two circles or in the form of a figure eight.

Always keep the safety factor in mind. No target should come in line with or cross another target or shooting position. Don't put a trail, target, or shooting position close enough behind another target to be in range of a ricochet arrow. Don't place targets on the brow of a hill where a high shot can go wild. Position targets, whenever possible, so that banks or hillsides can be utilized as backstops. In laying out up and downhill shots, make them easy to reach. Archery is a family sport, and to make an obstacle course of your range is a quick way to discourage potential members.

Target backstops, or butts, are usually made of baled hay, obtainable directly from farmers or from a grain-and-feed store. Old tire casings placed on the ground under the butts will keep them from absorbing excess moisture and rotting. Roofing paper, polyethylene or any type of plastic covering pinned over the top of the butts keeps out rain and prolongs their life. Butts should be wired to a stake in the rear so they can't be pushed over.

For an affluent club group, excelsior butts, although they are more expensive than straw or hay, are the longest lived and the best arrow stoppers. If baled hay is not available, you can substitute sandbags, large mounds of sod, or burlap bags stuffed with several layers of corrugated cardboard and sawdust between layers.

Target faces will last twice as long if pasted on corrugated cardboard. Use rubber cement rather than animal glue to keep rodents from chewing up the targets. They can then be pinned to the butts with large skewers made from coat-hanger wire.

Ground around the target butts, and especially in back of them, must be well cleared and raked to save time in locating stray arrows. Assign the care of each target position on your range to one of the members, and let them compete in fixing up these sites, keeping them clean and replacing worn target faces. The result will be a range well kept without placing too great a workload on anyone.

Individuals or prospective club groups can obtain much more detailed information on organizing, building ranges, running tournaments, etc., by writing to the national group of their choice. Addresses of these national group headquarters can be found in Chapter XII.

The N.F.A.A. allows the use of compound bows for both competition and hunting awards.

Chapter VIII

BOWHUNTING TACKLE

The growth of archery during the past thirty-five years to the status of a major sport is due in large part to one factor—increased interest in hunting with bows and arrows. Although various forms of target archery are increasingly popular, bowhunting is by far the largest branch of the sport.

There are several reasons for the popularity of bowhunting. Many sportsmen, having taken their share of game with a gun, now feel that hunting with the bow and arrow gives the game a better chance and is therefore more sporting. With a bow and arrow, hunters can better experience the ancient thrill of matching skill and knowledge with wild animals on a more equal basis than is possible with a gun.

Many have joined the ranks of bowhunters to escape crowded hunting conditions and to avoid the higher accident rate which prevails during firearms seasons. Still others use both firearms and the bow, taking advantage of the additional archery seasons to get more time afield and to sharpen their knowledge of game habits and hunting techniques. All these reasons can perhaps be summed up in one phrase: "more fun in the chase."

HUNTING BOWS

The modern-day bowhunter, when he takes to the woods, is equipped with a weapon far superior to that used by American Indians or any other races who lived by the bow.

Hunting bows are generally lighter and shorter than target bows. Recurved bows between 4 and 5½ feet long are the choice of many hunters because of their ease of handling in heavy cover or from a blind or an elevated stand. Recurved bows are more highly stressed than straight-limbed bows and so have added cast per draw weight. Despite these advantages, however, the compound bows developed in recent years have outstripped the recurve in popularity among bowhunters.

If you already participate in target or field archery, then selecting a hunting bow of suitable weight is a relatively simple matter. The draw weight of a conventional hunting bow should be about ten pounds greater than that of your target or field bow. Remember that in target or field archery, the bow remains in use for hours at a time, while in hunting situations you won't be taking many shots in the course of a day. If you have been using a 35-pound target bow, you should be able to work into a 45-pound hunting bow with no trouble. Of course, it will take a week or two of getting the shooting muscles used to the additional work.

The problem of changing from a target or beginner's bow to a heavier weight for hunting may seem difficult, but it must be remembered that muscles are built up by breaking them down. The weight lifter progresses by lifting weights that tire his muscles. He then rests them for a day or two and finds that he can now lift heavier weights because his muscles have responded by becoming stronger.

The same technique applies in moving up to heavier bows. One can never learn to pull heavier weights by continuing to use light bows; rather, he builds up to heavier bows by working out with them. The muscles used in drawing a bow are, for the most part, back muscles that are not generally developed, regardless of how strong one is in other ways.

The best way to train to pull a heavier bow is to shoot only as many arrows each day as can be done without excessive muscle fatigue. Shoot until you are tired but not so long that you cannot bring the bow to full draw, as this will lead to the hard-to-cure fault of snap shooting. You may take only a dozen shots at first, but this number can be increased each day or, better still, every

SOME BOWS AVAILABLE TO THE HUNTING ARCHER.

Colt Huntsman Hi-Power. *Hoyt Pro Hunter.* *Bear Kodiak.* *(Stedman Studio.)* *Bear Grizzly.* *(Stedman Studio.)*

other day, until you can handle fifty or sixty shots.

If you have never used a bow before and wish to purchase one for hunting, remember that it is a mistake to "overbow" yourself. Accuracy is far more important than sheer power. Get a bow you can handle—not one that handles you. In the days of all-wood bows, the hunter generally used a draw weight of between 65 and 75 pounds. Present-day composite bows, however, are so greatly improved over the wood types that it takes much less draw weight to do the job. For a man of average build, a good drawing weight for a first hunting bow is 45 pounds. For a woman or junior, 35 pounds would be about right. These weights are for conventional bows; a compound

Two-wheel compound bows. These require no tuning or adjustment and offer up to 50 percent let-off for greater ease of holding at full draw.

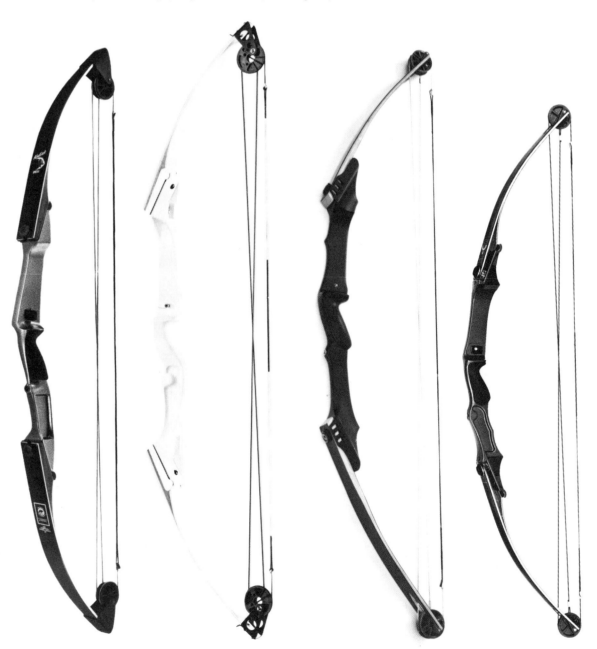

bow can generally be handled in a somewhat heavier draw weight.

These recommendations are for hunting game the size of deer or black bear. For smaller game such as rabbits or squirrels, a lighter bow is sufficient.

Before purchasing a hunting bow, be sure to check the game laws. Specifications for minimum hunting-bow weights vary from state to state, and you must be sure that you are within the law. Two states have set the minimum draw weight at 30 pounds. Most, however, call for more. And while some states specify actual draw weights, others simply state that the bow must be able to cast a hunting arrow a certain distance—130 yards, or 150 yards, etc.

In hunting the heavier and bigger-boned game animals such as elk, moose, caribou and grizzly bear, the hunting bow should not be less than 50 pounds, and 55 or 60 pounds is even better to insure proper penetration. I personally use a 65-pound bow for hunting all game; this weight, combined with razor-sharp arrows, has easily dispatched animals such as the Alaskan Kodiak bear, Asian tiger and African lion. The average hunter will probably not be in quest of such animals, but I include this information as a guidepost. If a 65-pound bow will kill a Kodiak bear, then 45 or 50 pounds should certainly be sufficient for a black bear.

In purchasing initial hunting equipment, it is not always advisable to get the most expensive bow available. Start with a medium-weight, medium-priced bow made by a recognized manufacturer. Always buy from a reputable dealer and make sure your bow carries the manufacturer's guarantee. After you have learned to shoot and have done some hunting, you will better know what your preference is in a hunting bow and can then invest in a top model.

I might add that, just as a good fisherman never goes on an extended fishing trip without a spare rod, so a bowhunter should never go on a hunt away from home without a spare bow. Accidents can happen, and one should be prepared.

HUNTING ARROWS

All three types of material—wood, glass, and aluminum—are now used for hunting arrows. Each material has its advantages and disadvantages. Wood shafts are inexpensive but break more easily and are subject to warpage. Glass arrows are tough and stay straight in all kinds of weather. Aluminum arrows are the most accurate.

There are two top choices in hunting arrows. Fiber glass-shafted arrows are becoming more popular every year. They will stand a great deal of abuse under hunting conditions and will stand just about any amount of bending up to the breaking point while retaining their original straightness. More recently, specially alloyed aluminum shafts have been introduced which are not only very closely matched in spine and weight but are also exceptionally strong and bend-resistant, making them ideal for hunting use.

Mention was made in Chapter I of the importance of selecting arrows in weights matched not only to the bow but also to the intended use—i.e., light for target shooting and heavy for bowhunting.

The reason for this difference, of course, is that the light arrow does not absorb nearly as much of the bow's energy as does the heavy one. Lightweight arrows are more inaccurate under hunting conditions because they are not as stable as the heavier shafts.

Hunting shots differ from practice or field shooting. In the former, the first shot counts most because in many instances an opportunity for a second shot does not occur. Your success or failure hinges upon that first shot, and it is here that the heavier shaft will aid your accuracy. Being loose and less sensitive to correct form, you have a better chance to score a hit, and you are more certain to win the trophy.

As hunting arrows have heavier shafts and heavier broadhead points than target arrows, they need larger fletching to steer this added weight correctly. They are also spined about 10 pounds stiffer than target arrows for a given bow weight. Feathers or vanes on hunting arrows are normally 5 or 5½ inches as compared to 2½- or 3-inch fletching on target arrows. Hunting fletch must be applied in a helical spiral. Some bowhunters like to use four feathers on their arrows. The one advantage of this is that there is no cock feather to be positioned—the arrow can be nocked on either side. The normal three-fletch arrow, however, is still the most popular style.

HUNTING POINTS

Many styles of broadheads are available at the present time. There are the two-edged blade (usually called a single-blade head), the three-bladed type, and the four-bladed type.

My personal advice to bowhunters has always been not to use single-blade broadheads for big game. Four-blade heads are best, as they have twice the cutting area of a single blade and more than a three-blade head, and thus are considerably more effective. Four-blade heads will cut arteries and other vessels, while other heads could slide by without touching these vital areas. Other advantages are that additional edges will increase hemorrhage for a quicker kill and will give additional penetration by making an incision which eliminates pinch on the arrow shaft, letting it "follow through" with greater ease. Four-blade heads are also easier to sharpen properly than are three-blade heads, particularly if one of the blades is of the replaceable type.

You can easily compare the cutting and penetration qualities of the various broadhead types by shooting them through several layers of heavy corrugated cardboard.

The first place to look for the qualities that make a good archer hunter is in his quiver. If his arrows are not keenly sharpened, either he is careless or someone has failed to impress upon him the fact that arrows have little shocking power and can only kill when razor sharp. Penetration alone is not enough, as dull heads will merely push tough-walled arteries aside in their squeeze through. It would be much better to have lightweight sharp arrows than dull heavy ones. Also, a 50-pound bow would be more deadly using sharp arrows than a 60-pound bow with dull ones.

SHARPENING HINTS

It is not difficult to sharpen broadheads if one remembers that it is merely the beveling down of two sides of a blade until they meet. Just because the sides are shiny and show signs of recent filing does not mean that the blade is sharp. Broadhead sharpness means that a stroke will shave hair off your arm.

The best cutting edge on a broadhead can be obtained by stroking the blade edges with a medium-grade, single-cut mill file. Stroke toward

THERE ARE MANY TYPES OF BROADHEADS ON THE MARKET.

These are three of the most popular:

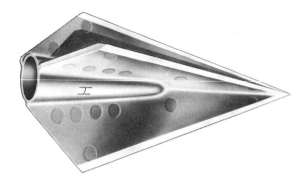

Hi-Standard 3-blade.

Colt Super Hilbre.

Bear Razorhead.

the point at the original bevel. The file stroke from the back of the head to the point has the same effect as a butcher's steel in removing the burr for best final cutting surface. The angle of the teeth on the file, combined with forward direction of the stroke, provide the shearing angle necessary to bring the very edge to its sharpest.

Holding the arrow in the left hand, stroke each cutting edge once and rotate the head between strokes. Do this five or six times on each side of each edge. The finishing stroke should be on the edge that is toward you. If the head has been dulled by shooting, it will probably be necessary to actually file the entire beveled edge before beginning the stroking operation. Do not file the tip to a long slender point, as this may cause it to curl when striking hard bone. The tip should be dubbed off, or rounded slightly, to a chisel point, which makes it much stronger.

Serrated and sawtooth edges on a broadhead should be avoided. While they look wicked, actually the teeth fill with hair, tallow, and tissue and thus impede clean cutting and penetration. In the case of broadheads with replaceable blades, always remove these auxiliary blades before sharpening the main blade edges.

Do not make the mistake of dulling sharp broadheads by letting them jostle together in a quiver, sticking extra arrows in the ground on a stand, or even snipping off grass or weed stems as you walk along. The heads must be very sharp when they hit game, and it is a waste of time to sharpen them if their keenness is not preserved.

Some type of hunting quiver that holds each

Hunting heads must be kept very sharp at all times. A flat mill file is one of the best means of accomplishing this.

A final broadhead inspection before the hunt.

arrow or arrowhead separately should be used. Examples of these are bow quivers, some hip hunting quivers and the St. Charles type of back quiver. It is also important to use a quiver which has a protective cowl or hood for the heads, both to preserve their sharp edges and to protect the archer from those edges.

Wiping broadheads with an oily cloth or applying a light coat of vaseline will not only keep rust from corroding sharp edges but will also aid in penetration.

An arrow which has been shot at game and recovered should not be put back in your quiver without first resharpening the broadhead. Your presence in the woods as a bowhunter morally obligates you to use the most efficient and hu-

mane instruments available. Sharp broadheads fulfill this need.

BOWHUNTING ACCESSORIES

Many bowhunters have found the bow quiver to be the best means of having arrows ready for fast action. Most models hold four arrows, although eight-arrow models are also available. I would never advise anyone to use a bow quiver that does not have a protective hood over the broadheads. Carrying well-sharpened heads without such protection can and has resulted in some nasty accidents. When using a bow quiver in rainy weather, a light plastic bag can be slipped over the feathered end of the arrows and held lightly in place with a rubber band. The bag can be pulled off instantly when necessary.

In some areas of the West and North, where the bowman often covers many miles in a day's hunt, where longer shots are the rule, and where game such as mule deer, antelope, caribou, and mountain sheep are the quarry, it is common practice to carry both a back quiver and a bow quiver. The bow quiver is ready for quick action, while the back quiver carries a reserve supply of arrows.

Smaller accessories that the average bowhunter will find handy, and perhaps indispensable, are bowstring silencers, compass, hunting knife, broadhead file, touch-up sharpener, game scent, a deer or other game call, arrow holder on the bow, binoculars, camouflage paste for hands and face, proper footwear, and inconspicuous or woods-blending clothing.

Various types of string silencers are available. One of the best is made of rubber in a three-pronged design. It is mounted by sliding it on over bowstring loops and positioning it at each end halfway between string nock and center of bow. These silencers eliminate string vibration and dampen the release "twang" to a whisper, avoiding unnecessary spooking of game.

The need for a compass is obvious. Suffice it to say that you should have a compass with you whenever you hunt in unfamiliar territory. Handy compasses for bowhunters are those which either pin onto the shirt pocket or sleeve or attach to bow or wrist with a strap. Incidentally, do not wait until you are lost before checking the compass.

Some sort of hunting knife is of course necessary, not only to dress out game but for such other sundries as building blinds and digging an arrow out of a tree. Many hunters depend entirely on a stout pocketknife, but still more prefer a belt knife, as these are built for more rugged use. There is available a bowhunting kit consisting of a good-quality hunting knife, a broadhead-sharpening file and carborundum stone for both knife and broadheads, all compactly carried in a leather belt sheath. At any rate, be sure you have

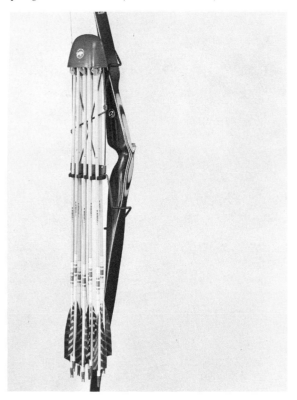

This bow quiver carries eight arrows and is mounted and detached from the bow by means of a coated spring steel bracket. (Stedman Studio.)

Another type of bow quiver having two slip-on brackets and a detachable hood. (Shakespeare Company Photo.)

a good flat mill file with you. And for occasional light touching up of broadheads, a small pocket-knife sharpener comes in handy.

More and more bowhunters use some form of commercial scent both to hide human odor from sharp, wild noses and in the hope that game might think he is another of their kind. The bowhunter has to take every advantage he can to defeat the highly tuned instincts of wild game.

A deer call is a good thing to have in your pocket. These calls don't always get results but, when they do, are well worth their modest price and light carrying weight. Many successful bow-

hunters never go out without one. Some type of varmint calls are also handy for the bowman interested in small-game hunting.

When hunting in nippy weather, an arrow holder is very convenient. These devices fit on the bow handle and hold an arrow in place ready to be drawn without the necessity of holding it there with the finger. They release their hold on the shaft as you start to draw and flip silently back out of the way.

Binoculars are an indispensable aid to the bowhunter, but he should pick a type geared to the terrain on which he is hunting. Binoculars are

The St. Charles hunting quiver. Its main feature is a hood that affords complete protection to the arrow fletching from brush and wet weather.

sold under the classifications of 6×30, 8×35, 7×50, etc. The first number indicates the magnification; the second, the diameter of the objective (front) lenses in millimeters. For eastern deer hunting, a pocket-size pair of 6×30s is good. For all-around use and particularly in mountain and plains country, a pair of 8×35s is probably most useful. The amount of area that binoculars will take in is called the "field of view." All good binoculars nowadays list the field of view (so many feet at 1,000 yards) with the other specifications. Pick the glasses which, other factors being equal, give you the greatest field of view. Good binoculars are expensive ($50 and up), but they will last a lifetime, and like any other equipment, the best quality will do the best job.

To the bowhunter, as to all other outdoorsmen,

proper footwear is second to nothing in importance. You cannot enjoy hunting if your feet are sore, wet, or cold. There are so many types of outdoor boots on the market that one can't begin to list the merits or shortcomings of them all. Just be sure you buy a reputable brand, get the type best suited to the terrain and weather conditions where you will hunt, and break them in well before your big hunting trip. Never start off on a hunt with new and untried footwear.

To break in leather boots properly, put them on, soak them thoroughly by sitting with your feet in a bucket of water, then wear them for several hours. Next dry them out thoroughly and apply a coat of boot grease. They are then ready for a day's hunt.

In dry weather, soft leather boots about 8 inches high are good. Just be sure they have some

The bigger the country the more important binoculars are to the bowhunter.

type of soles other than leather. The ordinary tennis shoe and the light, leather-topped basketball shoe are also excellent in these conditions.

In country where the weather or footing will be moist, and in fact for all-around use, it is hard to beat the "swamper," a rubber-bottomed, leather-topped boot. Swampers are quiet, light in weight, have good gripping soles, and they keep your feet dry in tundra, springs, or other damp ground. The use of felt or lamb's wool innersoles with these boots will greatly improve foot comfort, and by removing and drying the innersoles each night, you are assured of dry feet the next morning. The one thing such boots do not have is the extra ankle support needed in high-mountain country. For this type of hunting, specially countered leather boots are needed, and there are many brands of these available.

For blind-sitting in cold weather, felt shoes under arctics, fleece-lined flying boots, and the newer insulated rubber pacs are all good for keeping the feet warm, but the hunter must be content to do but little walking in these more cumbersome boots.

Whatever type of footwear you use, be sure they are roomy enough to accommodate heavy socks without binding. Two pairs of socks are better than one regardless of whether you are wearing warm-weather or cold-weather gear. In warm weather a pair of light dress socks under medium-weight wool socks are fine, and in cold weather the medium-weight wool can be replaced with heavier outer socks.

Clothing selected should be suitable for the region, season, and climate in which you hunt, and for the type of hunting you do. Bulky clothing which binds or is too heavy should be avoided. Many hunters make the mistake of wearing too much. If the hunter keeps moving, even though very slowly, as he will in still-hunting, much less clothing is necessary than if he spends most of his time stationary in a blind or on a stand.

In warm weather, a suit of camouflage material over underwear is usually just right. In cooler weather, loose layers of light wool or flannel under windproof and water-resistant outergarments are preferred. In cold weather, lightweight insulated underwear will regulate the body temperature without weighing you down. If still-hunting is combined with blind-sitting, an extra layer of clothing can be carried along in a light back pack.

A few of the most useful accessories for the bowhunter: extra bowstring, string silencers, compass, extra matches, a length of strong cord, emergency food kit, game call, sturdy hunting knife, file and whetstone.

Clothing of neutral colors helps the archer blend with his background. It has been proved conclusively that deer and many other wild animals are color blind. However, they certainly can distinguish between dark and light tones and pick up movement of the latter more readily than dark tones.

A bowhunter should aim to break up the telltale human outline and blend with his wooded background in tone or shade. For this purpose camouflage suits are unexcelled. There are several makes of these—most of them good. You can get very lightweight suits for warm weather and insulated suits for cool or cold weather. Some suits are even reversible, with a camouflage pattern on one side and bright red on the other, for the hunter who uses both bow and gun. If a camouflage suit isn't used, soft flannel or wool clothing in grays, browns, or greens is next best.

Many bowhunters also darken their faces with a cold-cream-base camouflage paste or with burnt cork. Those in the know do not camouflage themselves and then carry a highly varnished bow

Camouflage clothing may seem unnecessary . . .

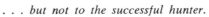

. . . but not to the successful hunter.

which can be spotted from afar. A coat of dull-finish lacquer or a camouflage bow-cover which slips on over the limbs are both available for hunting bows. Attention to small details helps to balance the odds which certainly are in favor of wild animals. Any sportsman planning to go after big game with a bow and arrow should not hesitate to take advantage of all possible breaks.

PRACTICE FOR BOWHUNTING

Regardless of how closely hunting arrows are matched to field or hunting-practice arrows, they do not always fly in the same way. One would assume that broadheads would cause arrows to drop faster in flight than field or hunting-practice points, but this is not true. It is essential to practice with the bow and arrows that will actually be used in hunting for some time before the season opens. Two weeks of daily warming up should be the minimum, and regular practice over a month's time is better.

Roving is a fine method for judging your aim

at various unknown distances. After you have become proficient in sending your roving broadheads to their marks, the sport will become more interesting if you use targets resembling the game you want to hunt. It is not good practice to shoot broadhead arrows at target faces pinned on bales, because the arrowheads will tear up the bales. Silhouette targets are easy to make and are more interesting to shoot at.

Let's say, for example, that you are interested in hunting deer. Draw the outline of a deer, as nearly life size as possible, on a sheet of corrugated cardboard. Once this first outline is cut out, it can be used as a pattern for others.

When you have a good supply cut out, double the thickness by stapling them together (or gluing them) in pairs. Then run a strip of masking tape along the top edge and press it down over each side. This will prolong the life of the targets by

A sandy bank makes an excellent backstop when practicing with hunting tackle. These archers shoot at a deer silhouette target . . .

preventing water from soaking in during rain or heavy dew.

Next, two short pieces of wire should be punched through each target about 2 inches down from the line of the back—one at the front shoulder and one at the rear ham. Your silhouettes are now ready to put in shooting position. By fastening a wire between two trees or stakes and attaching the target to this by means of the short lengths of wire, the silhouette can be placed at the normal height above the ground.

An alternate way of using these silhouettes is to use soft-wood stakes instead of wire, pounding the stakes into the ground far enough apart so that the front and rear edges of the target can be tacked to them with large-headed roofing nails.

In either case, be sure you have a safe arrow-stopping background. Targets can be placed against a hillside or against earth bunkers built behind the target positions. When placing the tar-

. . . and then check their hits and retrieve the arrows.

gets, try to lay out both uphill and downhill shots. Some of the shooting positions should necessitate kneeling, sitting, or canting the bow to get through or under brush or tree limbs. The harder you make it, the sharper your shooting will be.

Another type of broadhead target can be made from burlap bags stuffed with straw or excelsior. These will be about the size of a large deer's body and, like the corrugated silhouettes, can also be hung on wires.

If you live in a state where elevated shooting positions are allowed, you should practice shooting down at targets from various angles. Don't wait until you go hunting to get in such practice. Shooting down is very tricky until you get used to it, and you don't want to miss a possible once-in-a-lifetime chance at a big buck because you didn't know where to hold on him.

When practicing, never shoot at the entire target. You must train yourself to "pick a spot." If you don't do this on every practice shot, you will surely forget to do so when hunting.

Do not stop practicing when the season opens, even though you've shot daily for a month and feel you are in good form and ready for the hunt. It takes additional practice to keep that fine edge. A dozen or so warmup shots should be taken during the lunch break. The more limbered up and sure of yourself you are, the better will be your chances when the big opportunity presents itself.

The game silhouette target made of corrugated carton material is ideal for bowhunting practice.

Chapter IX

BOWHUNTING SMALL GAME

Some bowmen go after small game strictly as a means of sharpening up their shooting for larger game. Many others, however, hunt small game for its own excitement and fun, to say nothing of some fine eating.

There are a number of reasons why hunting small game holds such fascination. Hunting has a universal appeal for people of all ages. Youngsters not old enough to pull a strong bow or to be on their own in the woods enjoy hunting small game just as much as their elders enjoy the pursuit of larger game. And the youngster who starts out on small game will be a better hunter as he grows older.

Practically our entire country abounds with small game of some kind such as rabbits, hares, squirrels, gophers, woodchucks, raccoons, coyotes, fox, javelina, bobcats, game birds, and even frogs. Seasons are extensive. There is hardly a time of year when some small game, or animals classed as predators, are not in season.

No big outfitting with special equipment is necessary. Any bow can be used. About the only tackle needed which differs from that used in target or field archery are some blunt-tipped arrows —and in some cases flu-flu arrows. Small-game bowhunting is comparatively inexpensive too, in that the ammunition can often be reused. Arrows are not so easily lost, because shots are usually at fairly close range.

Rabbits are the number-one game animal in America. More archers, and gunners too, enjoy hunting rabbits than they do any other species of game. Rabbits are found east and west, north and south. There are cottontails, jackrabbits, snow-shoe hares and marsh rabbits. Their litters are large and, except for localized periods of thinning through disease, they make for consistently good hunting. Rabbits are easy to cook and good to eat. And they certainly afford plenty of tricky shooting.

The best arrows to use for most rabbits are those with blunt tips, which kill quickly by shock. Exceptions to this are the large blacktailed, white-tailed, and antelope jackrabbits of the western and southwestern sagebrush country. They are the largest and toughest specimens of the rabbit tribe and can take a lot of punishment. For this reason broadhead arrows are usually used.

Rabbit hunting is most fun when groups of hunters participate, spreading out and moving in a line through cover to flush out the game. This is an excellent archery-club activity. Some bowmen use beagles or similar rabbit chasers to stir up the action. When a hound gets a rabbit going, it is rare that the pursued and pursuer are close enough together to make a shot risky for the dog. Normally a jumped rabbit can stay far enough ahead so that the hunter has a good shot if and when the rabbit circles within range.

In quite a few states the snowshoe rabbit furnishes fine winter sport, with and without the aid of dogs. Single bowmen or a pair can stalk these rabbits, but such hunting is by no means easy. You must first learn to find them, which can be difficult since they are well-camouflaged if they choose to sit motionless.

Hunting tree squirrels, ground squirrels, and woodchucks is best done alone or perhaps with

Rabbits are the number-one game animal in America.

one partner. It is not only great sport in itself but is excellent practice for hunting larger game, as the same slow, quiet stalking and standing methods are employed.

Small game animals are quite difficult to bag with a bow. They are always on the alert and adept at outwitting a pursuer. Farmlands are exceptionally good places for such hunting, and a farmer will rarely refuse permission to hunt his woodlots, fence rows, and pastures.

Hunting frogs at night with a headlight is a lively sport. The main target is the bullfrog, which is the largest and most abundant species in this country. In the West the red-legged frog is also abundant and provides fine eating. Many archers tip their arrows with three-pronged, gig-type points for such nocturnal shooting.

VARMINT CALLING

Attracting game and predatory animals by means of a call is almost as old as hunting. Yet it is new to many modern-day sportsmen. This form of hunting is particularly suitable to the bowhunter, who must contrive to lure game to within the limited range of his bow.

All four-footed and winged animals classed as predators can be coaxed in with a call, and the curiosity, sex drive or grouping instinct of such nonpredatory animals as deer, elk, moose, ducks, geese, turkeys, and crows makes them susceptible as well.

Of all the forms of calling, however, varmint calling requires the least amount of skill. The calls imitate a small animal in distress. The panic cries of these animals are so varied that a hunter is sure to sound like one or another of them with the aid of an appropriate call.

Knowing the hunting country is important, and the area should be prescouted for best results. Information can often be gained from farmers and from the local game warden. Bowhunters should choose terrain that is a bit thicker than a rifleman would normally choose, as this allows for closer shooting. When calling in thick cover, it is important to keep a sharp lookout in all directions, as an animal may suddenly appear from an unexpected quarter.

Rolling hill country is not so conducive to close calling as flats, valleys, or washes. Your vantage point should be situated so you can easily watch a fairly large area. A small knoll or rise is a good spot. Don't sit on the very top, though. Sit far enough below the crest so you can see over it without showing your entire silhouette. For daylight hunting, early morning and evening offer the best chances, as these hours mark the peak of feeding by prey animals, and thus the peak of hunting activity by predators as well.

Calling alone will not lure varmints close enough for good results. Concealment is a prime factor in this game, and blinds are very helpful. Some terrain will offer enough natural cover, but camouflage clothing is necessary, and a head net is very useful.

After proper location and concealment, the most important factor is the wind. It should always blow in your face, never at your back. Varmints have sharp noses and don't like human scent.

*It takes a lot of woodsmanship to get close enough to a wild turkey
to shoot it with the bow. (B. Pearson Photo.)*

The javelina, or peccary, of our Southwest is an exciting small-game quarry for the bowhunter.

Many callers use commercial animal scents both to conceal their own odor and as an added attraction to the predators. Still days are better than windy days for calling. The piercing cry of a game call can be heard for a considerable distance. Therefore, when you change locations, move at least half a mile before calling again. Move every 20 or 30 minutes and cover plenty of country for best results.

As for the calling itself, the basic rabbit distress call is easily mastered. Commercial game calls are simple to manipulate, and all have instruction sheets outlining the proper technique. To do the job right, you actually need two calls, a long-range call and a close-in call, or squeaker. The long-range call is used until an animal is seen approaching the stand, at which time you switch to the squeaker to coax it in close. When the squeaker is just barely audible to you, it's just right for the brush lurker 100 yards away.

For calling all predators, other than bobcats, roughly 20 minutes is enough in one location. Predators like fox and coyotes come in without delay if they are coming at all. Bobcats, on the other hand, are slow, deliberate stalkers; sometimes it takes a half hour of calling to draw them in.

Gray fox are much easier to call than red fox, and in some areas the reds are very difficult to bring in. Raccoons respond very well to predator calls, as do hawks and owls. Do not kill the latter taloned hunters, though, regardless of what species they are. They do a great deal of good alive and none dead. If you must shoot them, do it with a camera.

Calling after dark is exciting and often more

Bobcats are wonderful game for archers in many parts of the country and make fine trophies.

Varmint calling is exciting and a good method of luring small game within bowhunting range.

Canadian guides use a birch-bark horn to call up bull moose.

productive than in daylight. When calling after nightfall, a headlamp is used. The light should be tilted up so that the area in front of you is barely illuminated. Swing the light steadily as you call. When ready for a shot, first swing the light down directly on the animal so that you can take proper aim.

Other hints for successful calling are: Camouflage your bow as well as yourself. Remove a bow quiver or back quiver when calling from a blind. Use string silencers. Don't carry anything in your pockets that may make noise when you move. If an animal is missed but not scared badly, it can sometimes be coaxed back with the call. When you get a chance for a shot, remember to get into position slowly so as not to scare the game away with a quick movement. Always kneel or stand while calling. If you are sitting down,

you'll never get up in time. Above all, develop patience. You may call at several locations with no results, but if you keep at it, sooner or later you'll get some action.

This is a great way to increase the range of bowhunting fun, and you will never forget the thrill of the first wild predator lured within bow range by the sound of your game call.

WING SHOOTING

Hunting birds such as pheasants, ducks, and wild turkeys with the bow and arrow certainly cannot be recommended as a reliable way to stock your larder. But, like all forms of bowhunting, bird shooting offers a special challenge and greater-than-usual satisfactions when occasional success is achieved.

Coyotes are among the predators who will respond to a varmint call.

At first thought, shooting birds in flight with an arrow may seem to be strictly a matter of pure luck. While this may be true in the case of an inexperienced archer, a bowman who really knows his equipment and how to use it can develop considerable skill in bird shooting.

The best way to prepare for such sport is by shooting corrugated cardboard disks about 10 or 12 inches in diameter. These disks are tossed into the air by a companion standing about 25 or 30 feet away from the shooter. The disks should be fairly heavy, made by gluing several pieces of cardboard together. About 1 inch is a good thickness. The disks are spun up by the edge so that the flat surface is toward the shooter. A black bull's-eye about 2 inches in diameter painted in the center of the disk helps greatly in aiming. For this practice, always pick an open spot such as a field or meadow, where the chances of a stray arrow hitting a person or a building are nil.

Arrows with blunt heads are usually used. Flu-

flu fletching on the arrows helps in retrieving them. This type of fletching consists of large untrimmed feathers glued completely around the shaft in a tight spiral. An arrow fletched in this fashion will fly at normal speed for 20 or 30 yards, after which wind resistance on the bushy feathers slows it abruptly and shortens its flight.

This type of shooting is actually easier than it appears to spectators. The secret is timing. The arrow should be drawn and released just as the disk reaches the peak of its rise and pauses slightly before starting to fall. Once an archer learns to time his draw and release in this manner, he can hit disks regularly. And for shooting at birds that rise in front of him, particularly on straightaway shots, this technique will pay off.

Quartering, or angled, shots at flying birds are perhaps encountered most frequently. As with the shotgun, an archer must lead his quarry in order to connect. Practice for such leads can again be

Raccoons have become almost as numerous as rabbits in some areas and are among the favorite targets of the small-game hunter.

Shooting at corrugated disks is the best preparation for wing shooting.

Wind resistance on the special flu-flu-type fletching slows the arrow rapidly after a normal flight of 35 or 40 yards.

done by two archers taking turns with the corrugated disks. One kneels behind a large tree, bank, or other cover and rolls the disks out one at a time, preferably down a slope or incline. The disks should roll past the shooter at a distance of 20 or 25 yards. Learning to lead is considerably harder than hitting the airborne disks, but with enough practice you can become fairly proficient at it.

No special bow is needed for bird hunting. The archer's regular hunting or field bow is fine. There are special bird points available for arrows, but regular broadheads work best. Flu-flu fletching on hunting arrows is, again, a big help.

A few of the variations possible in flu-flu-type fletching.

Grouse make a fine addition to the bowhunter's larder.

*Even the fast-flying waterfowl can occasionally be
downed with the bow.*

*Wild game birds such
as grouse and ptarmigan
are a welcome variation
in a hunting-camp menu.*

Chapter X

BOWHUNTING BIG GAME

The revival of bowhunting as a popular sport in America was due in large part to four men. The first of these were Maurice and Will Thompson, brothers who fought for the South in the Civil War. At the war's end they returned to their Georgia plantation only to find it in ruins. Maurice had been severely wounded in the fighting and was advised by his doctor to live in the open air if possible. The brothers had no means of livelihood and, as ex-Confederates, firearms were denied them. They took to the woods, where they lived chiefly on game killed with bows and arrows, which they had learned to make and use in their youth.

In 1877 a collection of Maurice's writings based on their life in the woods was published in book form under the title *The Witchery of Archery*. This fascinating volume proved very popular, and even now, almost a century later, is as interesting and entertaining as when it was written. These writings did a great deal toward awakening in this country an interest in archery as a sport.

The second pair of men to give impetus to American archery hunting were Dr. Saxton Pope and Arthur Young. Pope and Young were certainly influenced by the earlier writings of Maurice and Will Thompson, and, indeed, Dr. Pope acknowledges his debt to the brothers in his own writings. In addition, it became the lot of Dr. Pope, in 1911, to meet and help care for a small emaciated fellow named Ishi, last survivor of the Yana Indians of California. In turn, Ishi taught his benefactor many of the old Indian skills, not the least of which was the making of bows and arrows and their use in stalking game.

Arthur Young had learned archery from Will Compton, who in turn had learned it during many years spent among the Sioux Indians. These three—Dr. Pope, Will Compton, and Arthur Young—gravitated together through their mutual interest in archery and shot with Ishi until his death in 1916.

In the following years, Dr. Pope and Art Young made many hunts together. Notable among these was the taking of five grizzly bears in Wyoming. Three of these bears, the first grizzlies to be killed by modern archers, were mounted and became a representative group of this species in the California Academy of Science.

Young made two trips to Alaska, where he achieved such feats as bagging the first Kodiak bear and Dall sheep ever to fall to a modern American bowman.

My own interest in hunting with the bow and arrow was largely stimulated by a meeting and subsequent friendship with Art Young in 1927.

Dr. Pope wrote of their many adventures in a volume entitled *Hunting With the Bow and Arrow*. This book, first published in 1923, is probably the finest work available on archery hunting and was unquestionably the single most important factor in turning thousands of sportsmen to the use of the bow as a hunting weapon.

In the years following the publication of *Hunting With the Bow and Arrow*, sportsmen in various parts of the country began to take up this "new" sport. No one knows how many bowhunters there were in those early days, for until the formation of the National Field Archery Association in 1939 there was very little organization among them. They were individualists who hunted in the regular seasons and in competition with gun hunters.

The year 1934 marked the beginning of the trend toward separate seasons and areas for bowhunting. In that year Wisconsin set aside the first special bow-and-arrow deer season in the United States. A year later, Oregon also provided a separate bow season, and at the same time set aside the first special area for bowhunting only. Two years later, Pennsylvania designated a similar area. Michigan followed with the third special bowhunting area.

In the years following, the list of states providing similar seasons and areas increased. The last state to join the list was Kansas, which until 1965 did not have a large enough deer herd to justify open seasons. In that year it opened a special 45-day season for bowhunters as well as a first firearms season. Now all our states offer special bowhunting seasons, special areas, or both, for some form of game, and the bow is nationally recognized as an efficient and humane sporting arm.

WHAT MAKES A GOOD BOWHUNTER?

There are two main categories of bowhunters: those who enjoy the quest because it gives them more time out-of-doors, and those who are serious, dedicated hunting enthusiasts. The former

It is a good idea when hunting to spend some spare time each day keeping the shooting muscles limbered up and the eye sharp.

undoubtedly outnumber the latter, and for this casual type of bowhunter, stalking ability and knowledge of game habits are not necessary attributes. After all, any novice hunter can find someone who will show him where deer are moving, help him to build a blind, and then wait them out. Or he can drive around the woods roads himself until he sees where deer are moving through, and then come back later to hide and try to intercept them.

To the dedicated bowhunter, however, knowledge of game habits, skill with his arm plus stalking ability are definite requisites. For those who are serious enough to spend the necessary time practicing this art, the rewards are tremendous.

There are two other keys to successful bowhunting—provided of course that the foregoing requisites are met. First, there is one split second when your chances of success are best and you must instinctively choose that time to shoot.

To illustrate this point I can recall a hunt on the arctic ice pack in the spring of 1966. I was after polar bear, but in twenty-five days I had not had a chance at one, due largely to unfavorable weather conditions. Then the weather cleared and a bear was sighted traveling along a pressure ridge on the ice. Accompanied by my cameramen, we moved ahead hoping the bear would continue on his course so that we could set up an ambush for him. I found a place on a mound of ice where I would be out of sight if he came by on my side, and high enough to shoot over if he came through on the other side. The cameramen found a hiding place about 20 yards back to cover any action on film.

We spotted the bear coming toward us about a half mile away. He showed up dark against the light snow, shuffling along in an aimless way with his mind on a good seal dinner as he investigated hills of ice and cracks in the snow.

At first he appeared to be coming right by us at close range, but at about 400 yards he swerved away from the ridge and seemed to choose a

The right equipment and skill in its use are an important part of bowhunting success.

The result of a quick decision.

course through rough ice that would put him 100 yards away as he passed me.

I had to make a decision. It seemed best to move out in front of him, which I did when he went out of sight behind some ice. We again found cover, with the cameras back of me as before.

The bear came into sight very quickly. Three hundred yards, 200, 100 . . . on a course that would pass me at 20 yards or even closer.

But the wind was not good in our new position. At 50 yards the bear's nose went into the air and he stopped and looked toward us. Not sure, but suspicious, he turned sideways looking our way and sniffing. Having been charged by polar bear twice before on other hunts and at closer range than this, I felt sure that he was trying to make up his mind whether he should come for us or run off.

This was the moment of decision. I rose from behind my cover and released an arrow. It looked good all the way and hit with a resounding smack. Immediately a red area appeared in the right spot close to the shoulder. He went down in the loose snow recoiling from the hit and snapping at the arrow while lying on his side. Then he was back on his feet like a cat and took off over the pressure ridge and beyond some 100 yards, where he went down again in some rough ice, this time for good.

I am sure that if I had not taken the shot when

I did, no further opportunity would have presented itself, and the hunt would almost surely have ended without a trophy.

The second point is remembering to pick a certain spot on the animal at which to aim. Nine out of every ten deer shot at and missed by archers are missed simply because the hunter shot at the entire animal instead of concentrating on a tiny spot in the most vital area. This is extremely difficult to remember under the excitement of hunting and even if the hunter realizes its importance, he will often forget it at the crucial moment. Overcome this by getting into the habit of talking to yourself each time a chance is imminent. You have to tell yourself to "pick a spot" in order to be sure of doing so. Even the experts do this.

Other factors are involved, of course, but the above mentioned are the most essential to hunting success. In summation, there is only one best time to shoot, and it is learned only by experience. And if you shoot without picking a spot, you will most likely miss.

STILL-HUNTING AND STALKING

Hunting technique is more or less the same regardless of what species of game you are hunting. Only the nature of the country and climatic conditions will influence methods.

I believe it is true that anyone who can successfully stalk whitetail deer can be successful with any other big-game animal. Therefore, the following observations will focus largely on the deer family. The extensive range of deer in North America makes for greatly varying hunting conditions. In sections where deer are reasonably plentiful and the cover quite thick, as in many parts of the East and Southeast, and where hunters also are plentiful, stand-watching or blind-hunting and driving are the most popular methods. In more open country where the terrain is hilly or mountainous, still-hunting and stalking are the preferred methods.

Still-hunting simply means moving carefully through the woods where game can reasonably be expected and continuing until it is sighted.

The problem in hunting any game is to get within shooting distance. When an archer is within good rifle range, his work has just started. For the average bowhunter 35 yards is about the limit for accurate shooting, and few bowmen can claim many big-game kills beyond 50 yards. This means that if the archer wishes to be consistently successful, he must either sit in a blind and wait it out or he must learn how to stalk. Stalking is the culmination of still-hunting—the means by which the hunter closes to within range of his bow once the game has been sighted.

Experience is most necessary in learning to still-hunt and stalk, but there are some fundamentals which generally apply. In its broader sense this form of hunting involves a great deal more than being able to move through the woods quietly. The hunter must acquaint himself with animal behavior, tracks and other signs left by game, and its feeding and bedding habits, and he must know how best to take advantage of these factors. He should be able to look at country new to him and determine the most likely portion to concentrate on.

Almost every animal has some defect in its make-up which, if known to the hunter, may be turned to advantage. There are few wild animals all of whose senses are equally and acutely developed. For example, the bear is very keen nosed and hears quite well, but sees rather poorly. The mountain sheep is extremely keen eyed and has moderate smelling power, but doesn't pay much attention to sound. The deer has a very good sense of smell and hearing, but his eyesight, while excellent for moving objects, is not good for stationary or very slow-moving objects. Deer also are full of curiosity. Often when a deer hears a noise it will come closer and try to discover the source. The western mule deer has a habit of stopping, even when frightened, to look back just

Where you find acorns this thick the deer will not be far away.

Tracks tell tales, this one being the record of a black bear's passing not long ago.

before topping out over a hill or rise. This is the time the knowledgeable hunter can get in a good standing shot.

Whitetail deer have long been given the edge in intelligence over the western mule and blacktail deer. But within the past few decades the western deer has experienced greatly increased hunting pressure and has proved its ability not only to survive but to greatly extend its range despite heavy hunting.

Since the object of stalking is to get as close to an animal as possible before shooting, one has to think like a deer in order to get close to it and consequently one must try to understand what makes it think or react as it does.

Deer are trained from birth to hide, camouflage themselves and creep away from noise and dangerous scent. Yet they have courage enough to lie motionless and let a hunter pass them by if they think their position is good enough to escape detection.

Deer have three principal faculties for detecting the presence of enemies—a keen nose, sharp eyes, and sensitive ears. Of these three, the sense of smell is by far the principal one to be considered by the bowhunter. Second to this sense is the amazing ability to see objects in motion. These two extremely sharp senses, combined with a well-developed sense of hearing, serve to establish a protective screen around deer at all times. It normally extends well beyond reasonable range of the bow and arrow and is difficult to penetrate.

The bow and arrow as a hunting weapon has three weaknesses. First and most important is the short range of the weapon, which makes it necessary for the hunter to approach well within the protective screen of the animal in order to obtain a reasonable shot. Second is the exposed position and motion necessary to make a successful shot. Finally, the twang of the bowstring travels some six times faster than the arrow and gives the deer time to get out of the way. These animals often react involuntarily to such a sound and can leap clear of a well-directed arrow from as close range as 20 yards. In bowhunting nomenclature, this is called "jumping the string."

A good trick when the woods are dry and noisy is to slip a pair of heavy wool socks on over your hunting shoes. It deadens the noise of your movements considerably.

In still-hunting deer, the foregoing is of primary importance. The natural instinctive faculties of the deer and the inherent weaknesses of the bow create a chain of never-ending problems. The hunter must locate undisturbed deer, penetrate their natural instinctive barriers, and then at close range and often with little cover make considerable movement to take a shot without being seen or heard. Impossible? No, it can be done by bowmen who will take the time to learn the ancient art of stalking.

A serious hunter begins planning his hunt at least a couple of weeks before the season opens. When possible, visit the intended hunting area and look for trails linking feeding areas, drinking spots, shelter areas, and bedding places. Some research on the favorite foods and preferred cover of the species to be hunted is a prerequisite. Any large game country has heavier concentrations of animals in some sections than in others. This is due to several factors. Great areas of otherwise good cover may not furnish suitable food. Also, the fact that game was in one locality last week or last year does not necessarily mean

that it will be there this week or this year.

For instance, in the scrub-oak country of the North and Northeast sections of the United States, deer sometimes feed on acorns from early fall until late in the winter, often digging through a foot of snow to uncover them. On the other hand, in seasons when the acorn crop is poor, the deer may consume the available supply within a week or two. Under these conditions it would obviously be a waste of time to hunt the oak areas.

Guides and other residents of an area are often a great help in locating the best spots for game, but it is well not to depend solely on a guide who may not be entirely familiar with the limitations of bowhunting. It is safer to sift any information carefully and investigate yourself.

Check the woodlots and apple orchards close by where deer have been seen all summer, or travel the few extra miles necessary to get into rougher country, even if you don't know it very well. By hunting season the trophy bucks may have headed for tougher cover.

A hunting arrow should not be carried in the nocked position while still-hunting. If this hunter slipped, the soft leather stalking boot would offer little resistance to the sharp broadhead. (Laurence Lowry.)

The still-hunter should occasionally kneel and look under low limbs and through brush. The movements of an animal's legs can often be detected this way.

Author with a whitetail buck he tracked along an old logging trail.

After a hunting spot has been decided upon, the matter of *how* to hunt will be governed partly by the density of brush and cover. Some areas are entirely too dense for still-hunting even when the footing is comparatively quiet from recent rains.

Check for sites where you can get broadside views of animal trails. Perhaps the area has distinct wind patterns. Which way will you enter? How will you cross or skirt openings? Enter your hunting grounds against the wind if you can. If there is but little breeze, remember that air flows up the slopes when it is warm and into low places during the cool hours of the day.

Since the best times for still-hunting are early morning and late afternoon, when game is moving to or from feeding areas, stick to high ground most of the time. The still-hunter must always move directly into or quartering across the wind. A deer can seldom, if ever, be approached within bow range downwind.

Remember also that when a deer is about to bed down, he will travel into the wind for a short time before choosing a spot. When he does lie down, he will face his backtrack and rely on his eyes to see enemies downwind, and on his nose to sense danger from the opposite direction.

It is erroneous to believe that deer bed down for the entire day. Quite the contrary is true. Their movements are governed by their stom-achs, and when hungry, they seek food around their bedding grounds both day and night.

Usually deer do not bed alone, and yet, when in a group, they do not bed too closely together either. The beds are scattered somewhat for various lookouts, and their occupants lie so as to be looking in different directions. If you spot a bedded deer, unless it is a big old buck, you can be fairly sure there are others nearby. You must locate these others or you will not get any closer than your first sighting.

As has been said, still-hunting is traveling as quietly as possible until game is sighted. Stalking is approaching game to within shooting range.

In wooded country, assuming you have selected an area with the largest concentration of game, the best procedure is to walk game or cattle trails, or to pick routes that will allow progress with the least possible noise. By all means, go alone. Two people make twice as much noise, and noise must be kept to a minimum.

The whole purpose in still-hunting is to see game before it sees you. If you are sighted first, it is not likely that plans to get within shooting range will materialize. There are exceptions, however.

There is nothing magic about traveling quietly. It is a mechanical process of picking your footsteps carefully, keeping your balance, and going slowly. The only thrill greater than sighting game is to successfully stalk within bow range.

Game animals have no magic powers either, but the sharpness of their eyes, ears and nose create a real challenge to your woodsmanship. They are alerted by many cues that escape the average hunter. They know about the wingbeat of a grouse, for instance—whether it is merely flying into a tree or whether it has been flushed by an enemy. The chirp of a squirrel will tell them whether it is warning of an intruder or only engaging in squirrel talk, and woodpeckers, jays, and robins shriek an alarm signal that is quite familiar to game as well.

Only experience can teach you the difference in these alarms, and it is safest to pause for ten minutes or so whenever these birds or animals utter unusual calls. Game will forget about it after this length of time, and you may resume your progress.

These alarm signals can be used to your advantage also, as birds or animals frequently cry out when they have sighted the very game you are

Picking the right second for the shot and concentrating on the spot to be hit are the biggest factors in making hunting shots count.

hunting. Another reason to pause, look and listen.

Excellent periods of game movement occur just before and just after storms. Deer sense when storms are coming and move about more for intensive feeding, knowing that once they have a full stomach, they can wait out the storm in protective cover. During such a time they may be on the move at any time. Following a storm, feeding activity is again temporarily increased to make up for lost time.

When approaching open places where movements cannot be concealed, or very thick cover where it is impossible to get through without making noise, barge right ahead; get it over with. In open country where there are scattered clumps of cover, you can pick out what seem to be advantageous points of view ahead. Hurry to these positions, then carefully survey the surroundings. This method should be used in hilly areas where you have been exposed to whatever animals may be on the side of the hill nearest you. The idea is to be stationary while trying to catch sight of animals when they move.

A novice hunter will alarm considerable game as he moves along, and at least some of these animals will escape his scrutiny of the cover. Even

the finest of still-hunters will alert more game than he sees.

One autumn I was hunting mountain sheep in the back country of British Columbia. On arising one morning, I noticed that the weather looked questionable and asked Charley, my Indian guide, if he thought it would rain. The venerable redskin hesitated a moment and then sagely replied: "Me not know—no listen to radio last night."

So much for predicting the weather. The thing to remember is: Don't stay in camp on wet or stormy days. Deer do not always seek cover during light storms and may often be seen calmly feeding during a rain. Such days provide excellent opportunities for a silent approach. On wet or snowy days the deer has to rely chiefly on sight for protection, and this is sometimes dimmed by raindrops or snowflakes on its eyelashes. A beautiful, calm, clear day is a joy to spend in the woods with a bow, but a stormy, blustery day is far better in many ways, for then you travel noiselessly and shoot with a silent string.

Windy days are also good for the still-hunter and are often his only chance when a dry spell makes footing noisy. The reason, of course, is that the wind rustling through leaves and bushes

*Good tracking snow
provided a big help
to the stalkers of this
large mountain lion.*

drowns out the noise made by walking. However, animals seem to sense this and are especially alert on windy days. During such weather deer are likely to be found on the sheltered side of ridges and ledges or in thick swamp or brush.

During a spell of dry weather when the going is noisy, seek out a section that is not too open and where vision is limited to 50 or 60 yards at best. Start out walking and make all the noise you like. Travel right along, trying to appear as unconcerned as possible. However, be alert and have an arrow ready. It is not unusual for deer, even bucks, to stand and look as you pass by. Bird shooters who have hunted in deer country tell of numerous occasions when deer have stood so close they have all but run over them. The reason for this seems to be that when hunting birds you do not sneak along in the crouching position that indicates so clearly that you are a hunter. Some wild game, deer especially, are curious enough to do the unusual when they come upon a human behaving in an entirely ordinary manner.

In the northern sections or in higher elevations of game country a good tracking snow is helpful. An ideal snowfall is 2 to 6 inches, enough to cover the ground yet not enough to hamper the hunter's actions. Increased visibility after a snowfall plus the fact that game will be seeking food

after the storm also work to the advantage of the hunter.

Of all the rules used by successful still-hunters, three stand out: Never step on anything you can step over, take a few steps at a time and then stop, and train your eyes to see detail. The first will aid in noiseless approach. The second may give you the advantage of seeing the animal before it sees you—taking advantage of the fact that while game is quick to see movement, it does not readily pick out motionless objects from the rest of the scenery. If your scent is not detected and you remain perfectly still even in the open, your presence will often go unnoticed. When the game is seen first, the advantage reverts to the hunter—he can plan the pursuit instead of hunting by luck. The third rule may also allow you to spot the animal first.

Do not spend too much time looking in open areas for deer. Look at small openings between trees and through brush and try to pick out a single part of a deer—perhaps his ears, head, legs, or rump. A horizontal line with one end rounded may be the back of a deer. Don't make the mistake of watching only ahead. Train your eyes back and forth and from side to side over every bit of cover. *See* what you are looking at. If you spot an object which might be part of a deer,

When the hunters have a long way to go to reach camp or their car this is one good way of taking out the game.

study it with your binoculars. Look for a patch of color out of place in its surroundings. Get down on your hands and knees and look under low branches now and then where the white portions of a deer's legs might be seen. Be especially alert to any movements, no matter how small. The flick of an ear or the motion of a tail may focus your attention on a spot, and suddenly the entire outline of an animal will take shape. Look back once in a while. Deer are crafty and sometimes will hide as you walk by and then sneak out behind you.

You might possibly get a good shot during the middle of the day by following along the sunny slope of a ridge or hill about one third of the way down from the top. It is even possible in such situations to spot bedded deer before they spot you. Here is where seeing instead of just looking is important. In the mountains one of the favorite haunts of big bucks is under the steep rimrocks

along ridges. Another is in aspen thickets at the head of steep gullies. Moving slowly along just below the crest, keeping to cover as much as possible, carefully scan every foot of ground ahead and below.

Although a deer's nose is its chief protection against the bowhunter in open cover, it depends more upon its eyes to detect intruders. The hunter must match this by his own ability to see; here is where good binoculars are especially handy. When moving deer are spotted from high ground, the hunter can watch them long enough to determine their general line of travel and then circle around on the downwind side in the hope of setting up an ambush.

In some areas the still-hunter finds prospects best on the fringe of farmlands in early morning and late afternoon, especially around large orchards near woodlands.

The hour after dawn is the best time of all for

*A stick tied to the antlers
serves as a good lever for
this fine buck.*

still-hunting deer. After feeding undisturbed most of the night, they move toward bedding, ground-feeding as they go. They are less wary and also keep their heads down in those early hours more than at any other time of day.

Still-hunting, while essentially an individual endeavor, can often be successfully done by a pair of hunters. Not just any pair of hunters. They must be companions who really enjoy hunting together and who know pretty well what the other's movements will be. Hunting as a team, they can take turns quietly flushing game from heavy cover while the other posts himself at some likely escape route as the animal tries to sneak away. It is like a small drive except that the hunter, working through the cover, will quietly still-hunt game toward his partner.

This often affords exciting opportunities that one hunter cannot take advantage of alone. Each stretch of cover offers its special problem. The key to success is being able to maintain contact with the partner periodically so that new plans can be formulated. Two hunters in a region fairly strange to them can find a respectable amount of game by coordinating their movements.

When hunting in country with brushy draws, coulees, or ravines, one hunter can progress directly up (or down) the middle to flush game out without badly frightening it while his companion walks the side of the hill and slightly in advance of the lower hunter, watching for animals trying to work out over the side or ahead of the flusher.

When spotting an animal some distance away,

For a short haul the bow itself can be used to facilitate dragging in the game.

one hunter can take cover and circle around while the other stays in view and acts as a decoy, holding the animal's interest but not getting so close as to scare it off. When an animal is occupied in watching an enemy in one direction, it is easier to approach from another angle.

Two hunting companions working toward a mutual success in this way are enjoying one of the most sportsmanlike and rewarding forms of hunting.

A stalk cannot be planned at home or in camp. Every situation presents different problems, and the hunter must analyze each problem as it arises. It may be wise for the stalker to make a wide detour around thick brush, even if he temporarily loses sight of his quarry. Dry leaves, dry limbs or twigs, and gravel are difficult to cope with, and shortcuts are usually fatal mistakes.

Most game animals are very sensitive to ground vibration. This means that as you get close to one in a final stalk, it is necessary to move not only soundlessly but without jar. The best way to accomplish this is to keep the body weight completely on one foot while advancing the other, and setting it down by first touching the ball of the foot to the ground and then the heel. The Indians learned to stalk in this fashion and were masters at it.

A stalking hunter, like a bobcat, should always use every available bit of cover, for it helps break up that telltale silhouette. When you have made a stalk to within bow range, it is wise to shoot from behind whatever cover is available. Whenever possible, draw and shoot when the animal's head is turned away from you, so that the necessary movements of your draw and release will not be readily detected.

Another trick to remember is that a deer usually switches its tail just before raising its head to look around. When you are trying to close the gap on a feeding deer, watch its tail and freeze when you see it move.

When a deer is located and a stalk has begun, always keep a close watch for other deer that are usually standing unnoticed in the vicinity. It is quite possible for a deer you do not see to warn the one you are after. If a deer should discover you before you are ready, but is within range for a shot, slowly and with as nearly imperceptible movements as possible, work yourself into a shooting position, draw and shoot. If you don't

take this chance, it is quite likely that you won't get another.

To sum up the basics of still-hunting and stalking, here are the rules of the successful bowman:

1. Never step on anything you can step over.
2. Do not move continuously. Take a few steps, stop, look, and listen. See your quarry before it sees you. Take short steps.
3. Train your eyes to see detail. Seldom will you see the whole animal at first, only part of it.
4. Hunt into or across the wind.
5. Avoid all unnecessary movements.
6. Whenever possible, time your shots to coincide with natural noises or when the animal's head is down. This will help prevent him from seeing your movements and jumping at the sound of your bowstring.
7. When working up on a feeding deer, move when it moves and watch its tail.
8. Keep cool and don't be in a hurry.
9. Scan the area close to you—a second deer may be watching you pass.
10. Check the wind direction carefully before beginning a stalk.
11. Avoid carrying a nocked arrow while on unsafe footing.
12. Know your capabilities. Stalk to within a good shooting distance.
13. In contrast to instructions to hunt slowly and deliberately, there are times to throw caution to the winds and run just as fast as possible to get to a place where a traveling animal may pass within bowshot.

Stalking is tough work both mentally and physically. But you will develop patience. You will use muscles you didn't know existed. Your mouth will be dry. You will sweat and silently curse, and you can never relax. But at last, when you've made a successful stalk, you will know beyond a doubt why it is called hunting's greatest thrill. To best a big-game animal in its own habitat is a satisfaction unexcelled in the field of sport.

PROPER USE OF BLINDS

Bowhunting offers the greatest chance of success to the hunter who stays in one place and lets the game come to him. Merely choosing a spot at random in the woods and waiting there hoping a

The mountain sheep makes a worthwhile trophy for the patient and skillful hunter.

deer comes along, however, is trusting too much to luck. Rather, choose an area frequented regularly by the animals and be there at the right times of day, immobile and properly concealed.

Again, preseason scouting of your intended hunting territory is essential. Fresh game sign-tracks, droppings, beds, pawed areas, and brush or tree rubs are the indicators to look for. Trails mean little without fresh tracks. By close examination it is easy to determine how fresh the various game signs are.

A blind should be built overlooking either a frequented feeding area or travel routes between feeding and bedding areas. The blind serves as a hiding place from which to ambush approaching game and must be situated so as to blend with the background. Do not build it close beside a trail. Pick a spot 20 or 30 yards to one side. It must also be situated in accordance with the prevailing wind direction. It is useless to sit in a blind with your scent blowing in the direction from which game is most likely to appear. If a really good spot is found, it is best to build two blinds, one on either side of the trail, so that no matter which way the wind is blowing, you will not be upwind. In extremely dry weather another good situation

for a blind is in a low, well-watered area where the animals will come to avoid the heat and to drink.

Avoid building blinds overlooking a large field or clearing. You may see game, but the shots would be too long. Plan for a close shot by pinpointing access routes to and from fields or clearings, and choose a stand well back in the woods.

As to the blind itself, there are several variations depending on the region you are hunting, but certain rules apply regardless of what type you use. The blind does not have to be either extremely large or particularly solid. It should be just large enough in diameter not to constrict the hunter's movements and should be constructed sparsely rather than with dense walls. Its main purpose is to disguise the occupant, break up his silhouette and blend it into the general background. If the hunter is properly camouflaged with dull or mottled clothing, the blind serves its purpose if it merely blurs his outlines.

The most important points to remember in constructing a blind are these: (a) Always use material natural to the area. (b) Do not build the blind so high that you cannot readily see over it in any direction. (c) It is more important to have

A view showing how the bow can be held in readiness across forked sticks.

good cover behind you than in front.

Do not haul in an assortment of logs, limbs or brush and pile them up in a wall. This is an easy way to get blind building material, but a wary buck will instantly recognize such a structure as being out of place and will steer clear of it. Similarly, the bowman who cuts a bunch of evergreen limbs and sticks them up in a grove of aspens or in a brush thicket is advertising rather than concealing his presence.

It takes patience to wait in a blind for two or three hours. One has to be comfortable both in position and dress to withstand the long periods of silent watching. Building the proper type of blind in which a sitting position is possible will take care of the first problem. Wearing clothing suitable for the weather will take care of the second. A small cushion or pillow can relieve the discomfort of sitting in one position for an hour or two at a time.

Game has a disconcerting habit of appearing from the least expected direction. In order to shift position without noise, it is wise to brush up all leaves and twigs from the ground inside the blind. Be sure to leave enough room between you and the walls of the blind so that you can turn in any direction without impeding the bow. If the blind is situated underneath trees, check for overhanging limbs or branches that might catch a bow tip.

Cut two forked branches about 1½ feet long. Point the unforked ends and push them into the ground a couple of feet apart in front of your sitting position. You can then rest your bow limbs horizontally in the forks. With an arrow nocked and ready on the string, the bow is in position to be quietly lifted to shooting elevation.

There are two invaluable tools for the blind-building hunter. One is a machete—that long-bladed knife much used in the tropics—carried in a belt sheath. It is obtainable through a variety of sources, including army-surplus stores, for about $5. Cut the blade down to about 12 inches in length. The machete is far handier than a hatchet for this particular type of work. The other tool is a small folding trench shovel, also available at army-surplus stores.

The two most effective kinds of blinds for any game are those that place the hunter below or above the animals' alert zone. A ground blind can sometimes be greatly improved by digging a hole 2 feet deep and 2 feet across. By sitting on the ground with his legs in the hole, the hunter is much less exposed and the walls of the blind need then be only a short distance aboveground. Shots can be made from such a blind by either rising slowly as the bow is drawn or from a kneeling position on the edge of the hole. Never try to shoot through holes in a blind; always shoot over the blind.

When a blind is completed, the bowhunter should try a few practice shots in all directions to make sure he has clear shooting lanes and that he can shoot without becoming entangled in the blind. Often limbs or twigs will have to be removed outside the blind to obtain clear shooting lanes.

An excellent ambush may be made by cleaning out a space in the middle of an existing brush pile or downfall without disturbing the outside. Odd spaces between the logs or limbs can be lightly filled with branches, clumps of tall grass, or other plants in the immediate area. When using limbs of bushes or trees in the walls of a blind, place them so that the leaves have their normal upward face toward the outside. Branches whose leaves show their undersurfaces in an unnatural position may make game suspicious.

Another good type of blind can be made by hollowing out the center of a bushy clump of small willows or similar growth and sitting inside the clump on a box or small portable seat. You can see out through such a clump and still be

Bengal tiger shot by the author in India from an elevated platform, or machan.

On the antelope plains of the West, blinds are constructed near waterholes, using the sagebrush which grows nearby.

fairly well concealed. Do not try this with brush over 4 feet high, as you have to rise and shoot over it when the chance comes.

Undoubtedly the most effective blinds of all are those elevated above ground level in trees or on platforms. Such stands can be either natural or one of the many portable commercial models available. Regardless of the type used, the secret of long watches is comfort. This means being dressed for the weather and having a comfortable seat.

It is generally assumed that in shooting down from an elevated position, arrows fly higher and considerable correction must be made. This is not true. The difference at 40 yards is but a few inches higher. Any correction based on the flatter trajectory and made by aiming lower will most likely result in a very low hit or a complete miss.

This is not to say that if a bowsight or the gap system is used, corrections will not have to be made. Only practice will solve this problem. If you find it necessary to aim lower, the reason is not that the arrow flight is flatter, but rather that your shooting form is different when you bend to shoot below the usual horizontal. An instinctive shooter, trained to shoot from any position, makes no corrections shooting up or down at customary hunting range.

An elevated stand has the disadvantage of a confined shooting space in addition to the possible danger of a fall. The safety angle can be improved by securely fastening the stand platform and by connecting a safety line from self to tree.

Outweighing the disadvantages are several important advantages: The game is seen before it senses danger; your scent is usually carried by air currents above their level, full concealment is not so crucial, and there is a greater possibility of a second shot.

Shooting from an elevated tree stand.

Most commercial tree stands are readily portable and easily erected.

An elevated stand has definite advantages for the bowhunter.

Important keys to successful stand hunting are (a) choosing a location with a good view of either approaching or passing trails, (b) positioning your stand off to one side of any trail, rather than directly over it, (c) using a rope or cord for raising the bow and arrows after you have climbed up (this same cord can then be used as your safety line), (d) laying an old piece of carpet or other nonskid material on the stand platform for quietness and secure footing, (e) making sure you have cleared shooting lanes, and (f) shooting as heavy a bow as you can handle accurately. An animal's body depth is greater than its width, and angled shots have to penetrate more deeply than those taken on the level.

It is not necessary to get too high off the ground—10 to 15 feet is enough to place you above the normal scent and vision line of the game, and still allow for accurate placement of shots.

The best times to hunt from either a blind or tree stand are the two or three hours after daylight and before dark, when game is most active. But remember, more deer are taken by archers who have reconnoitered the territory and are well acquainted with the deer runways, feeding areas, escape cover, the effect wind and terrain have on the travel of the animals, and then place their blinds or stands accordingly.

If you are hunting in an area where you will want to make temporary watching places, a rectangular piece of camouflage netting material, about 3 feet by 6 feet with tie strings fastened at the corners, can be folded and carried in a pocket. Tied to trees or brush, this provides fast and excellent concealment.

The value of a blind can be destroyed by carelessness in approaches and departures. The hunter who uses the same route each time he comes into and leaves the blind, soon has a clearly defined path. To avoid this, take a slightly different route each time and do as little damage to the vegetation as possible.

Don't take a bright object such as a thermos bottle into a blind without covering it with something. Sun glinting on a shiny surface could spook an approaching animal. The man who hunts consistently from blinds should have several in various locations so that he is not sitting in the same one all the time. Using a blind only every other day will keep human scent from saturating the area.

Many hunters believe they are being quiet in a blind, when actually they are turning and twisting about in a continual effort to watch all directions where game might appear. Alertness is necessary, but it should not be exercised at the expense of quietness. Any movement, such as turning the head, should be made slowly and deliberately. Remember that it is movement the game detects most easily.

If you have been still-hunting and suddenly a horde of other hunters invade your area, the best solution is to turn to blind-hunting. The deer will not scatter any farther than they have to and will usually return to favored feeding grounds even if they have to sneak around hunters to do so. Still-hunting under such conditions is out of the question, and even organized drives would not be productive. Hunting from a blind in such a situation is a dawn-to-dusk proposition if the hunter is to be successful. If the hunter has scouted the area well before season, he will know some of the best watching points to use while other hunters are infiltrating the woods. Such watching takes a great deal of patience. One is always tempted to find a better location, and as the hours wear along he feels the urge more strongly.

The fact is, however, that moving about completely defeats the watcher's purposes. The longer you stick to a good stand, the greater your

An arrow holder is a handy gadget, particularly in cold weather. It releases its grip on the shaft when the arrow is drawn. (Stedman Studio.)

Bob Lee with a record-class barren ground caribou from Alaska. (Wing Archery Photo.)

chances of seeing game. Many a shot at a fine buck has been missed because the hunter got restless and decided to move just as the deer was approaching his blind.

An excellent combination hunting method is to use a blind or tree stand in the early morning, still-hunt during midday, and retire to the blind or stand again in the late afternoon.

DRIVING DEER

Driving deer is widely practiced by bowhunters in the eastern and southeastern states. In parts of the Southeast the cover is so thick that the use of dogs is legal and the chief method of hunting. When hunters themselves are to be the "hounds" on a drive, the number can vary from half a dozen to fifty or more. One thing to keep in mind is that the more men involved the more unwieldy the process. One or more of the crowd can foul up the operation through misinformation or carelessness.

A dozen to twenty hunters is a good number for driving deer. This makes an excellent weekend project for the members of an archery club who live near suitable cover. In smaller groups the number of standers to drivers can be disproportionate. For example, where the area to be driven is roughly wedge-shaped with its point downwind, there should be more drivers than standers; but if the large end of the area is downwind, there should be more standers and fewer drivers.

Drivers should be posted between 50 and 100 yards apart. This distance will vary with the thickness of the cover, but at any rate, the driver should be able to keep track of the man on either side of him by sight as well as by sound. This will prevent animals from sneaking back undetected through the line of drivers. Unlike still-hunting, the drivers keep off the game trails and move through the heaviest cover, advancing crosswind whenever possible and making just enough noise to maintain proper spacing and a straight line.

After each hunting shot the broadhead should be carefully resharpened. Hunting heads must be kept sharp at all times.

Baying like hounds at intervals is effective. Because of the habit of deer, particularly big bucks, to lie low until a drive has passed, it behooves the drivers to keep a sharp eye and be ready to shoot at all times.

Standers should position themselves with one thought uppermost: What are the most likely routes for game to take in sneaking away from the disturbance?

Rules for staging successful deer drives are these: Only one man should be in charge. The maxim about "Too many chiefs and not enough Indians" applies here.

Keep the area small. Trying to cover too much

ground will only leave escape routes. A drive of a half mile is usually far more successful than one of a mile. Game can be driven only so far along a straight route before they turn out to seek safety elsewhere. It is also very difficult for a line of drivers to hold correct spacing and timing over a large area.

The group should be divided, as equally as conditions warrant, into drivers and standers, alternating the positions on each drive. Standers should be posted along the sides of the last portion of the area to be driven, as well as across the end. It must be impressed on the line of drivers that they go slowly and keep in sight of the men

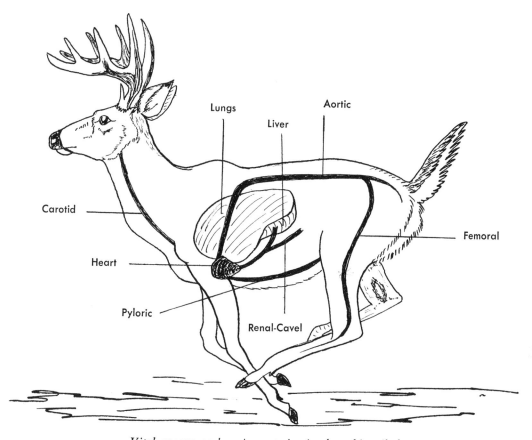

Vital organs and major arteries in the whitetail deer.

on both sides, and on the standers that they not move around but stay in position until the drive is completed. It is important that the standers take their positions as silently as possible and remain quiet. Wind direction and lay of the land will always determine the drive direction.

WHERE TO HIT LARGE GAME

Much has been said about where to shoot large game with an arrow. It is general knowledge that a hit anywhere in the chest cavity, or that portion of the body enclosed by the rib cage, results in the quickest and cleanest kills.

Lung shots are the easiest and most effective of all for the archer. The lungs fill much of the forward chest cavity and hence are the largest fatal area available. These organs consist of spongy cells filled with blood which are served by a network of large arteries plus thousands of smaller blood vessels. A sharp arrowhead cutting through these cells will not cause sudden death unless a major artery leading to the heart is severed in the process. However, in almost every case a lung-shot deer, or any other large animal, will not go far.

Heart shots are always fatal, but the heart is a small target for the archer unless the shot is taken at very close range. Whenever possible, of course, aim for the heart "spot" (just behind the front leg and low). Hunting shots have a tendency to go high for most archers, and a shot aimed at the heart which goes a bit high will hit the lungs.

The fastest way to down big game is to cut an artery close to the heart. A large arterial system serves all parts of an animal's body. When any one of these major vessels is cleanly cut, it is fatal. Only the largest arteries are shown in the accompanying sketch of vital organs.

A hit in the liver, like a lung shot, can be almost instantly fatal. However, if you do not cut the large arteries which serve the liver and spleen the animal may move some distance before suc-

Author with spiral-horned kudu from Portuguese East Africa. This animal is larger than our native elk.

cumbing. If you've hit a deer through the middle of the body, don't give up the trail. A liver shot, even if the vessels are not severed, will usually put an animal down in the first available cover.

These are the most vital spots in deer and other large game. There are certain other areas in the body where a hit will prove either instantly fatal or fatal within short periods of time. A hit in the brain is of course immediately fatal, but this is most certainly a lucky shot and should not be attempted. A hit anywhere in the spine, while it will instantly down an animal, usually occurs entirely by accident.

The stomach is located in back of the diaphragm, which separates the chest cavity from the abdominal, or body, cavity. Any hit in the stomach area usually causes much the same reaction as a liver shot. There will be little or no external bleeding unless an artery near the surface is cut. Treat a shot of this nature as you would a liver shot, but wait even longer before starting to trail your game.

A shot through the rear hams which cuts the femoral artery usually causes death very quickly.

Any shot angled from the rear in which the arrow goes in behind the ribs and ranges forward to the chest cavity is usually fatal. This is one of the best shots to take while hunting from a blind: Let the animal walk slightly past you before you rise slowly to shoot.

When a hit is made in the leg or any other part of the body where arteries are small, it is best to keep the animal up and moving. This is done not by swift pursuit but by pressing just enough so that it cannot bed down. If the game has a chance to rest, the blood may coagulate and bleeding will stop. This applies only when blood vessels near the skin surface are cut and the air hastens coagulation. Internal arterial wounds bleed freely and result in hemorrhage, even though little blood is shed externally.

I remember an incident from my early bow-hunting years in connection with trailing and finding a hit deer. It happened in the Allegan State Forest in Michigan's lower peninsula, where many fine bucks roamed in those days. Late one evening a hunting acquaintance of mine was fortunate enough to get a good hit on a huge antlered whitetail. Unfortunately, however, it was a Sunday evening and the hunter had to be back on his job in Detroit the following morning.

Regulations required that all game taken in the area be checked out at the Swan Creek Wildlife Station by the conservation officers in charge. The hunter decided to report his hit to the officers and try to enlist their help in finding his buck the next day. Thinking that he should have some evidence of having hit a deer, he broke an arrow in two, rubbed the rear half with blood from the trail, and presented it to them as evidence.

The following morning the conservation officers went to the location the hunter had pointed out, found the blood trail, and in a short time the big buck. However, upon dressing it out, they found that the front half of an arrow found in the deer did not match up with the rear half the hunter had given them!

The officers took the buck back to the station and notified the hunter that they had indeed found a nice buck where he said he had shot one, but doubted that the deer they found was his. When they explained the nonmatching arrow halves the hunter was obliged to confess his stratagem, whereupon they commented that as he had lied to them earlier, perhaps he was lying again in order to claim a deer that wasn't really his.

The hunter had to make a special trip back to Allegan, accompanied by an officer, and comb the scene of the hit in a painstaking search for the legitimate half of his arrow. Fortunately, he found it and was able to claim his prize.

Regardless of where you think the arrow hit, do not follow your game immediately (the one exception having been stated earlier). Mark the line of flight by sight and sound.

After a few minutes, walk quietly to where the animal was standing when the arrow hit. Look for blood signs, but don't be disappointed if they aren't immediately found. Game often takes off so fast after being hit that blood signs will not show up for the first 20 to 30 yards. Look also for hair cut off when the arrow hit. This can be a good clue as to just where the arrow entered the animal's body. For example, hair from high on the body will be dark and coarse with very dark tips; from the middle of the body or lung area, medium-brown without dark tips; and from low on the body, as in a stomach hit, much lighter and shorter.

When blood signs are found, light, frothy blood means a hit either in the lungs or in the carotid arteries of the neck. Bright-red blood without froth indicates arterial bleeding. Very dark blood indicates a liver hit or venous bleeding. Greenish or yellowish matter mixed with blood means a hit far back through the stomach or intestines. A shot in the intestines is a poor one, but many deer have nevertheless been killed by such a shot. If one of the arteries serving this area is cut, your chance of finding the game is good. The blood trail, however, will be insignificant.

After a hit, if you can see the animal lying prone within sight and not moving, you can slowly work up to it with another arrow ready on the string. If you cannot see the game, regardless of where you think it was hit or how good the blood signs, wait at least half to three quarters of an hour before trailing. The one exception to this would occur if a heavy snowfall or rain threatened to wipe out the trail. On shots that may have hit the liver, stomach, or intestines, it is best to wait even longer, if conditions warrant, before starting to trail. Many hit animals have been lost because the hunter was too impatient.

Again I want to stress that dull broadheads will halve the chance of a fatal hit. Use a multiple-blade head that will cut a large hole and create a better blood trail. A surgeon would not consider using a dull scalpel; the serious bowhunter should be just as particular about the condition of broadheads. It is imperative that they be as sharp as you can possibly make them.

Speaking of proper hits and finding game reminds me of another incident which took place years ago when my archery business was in Detroit. A group of bowhunting "addicts" were in the habit of gathering in my office of an evening to swap hunting yarns, information on equipment, etc.

One evening a newcomer dropped in and, listening to the talk, became extremely interested in the subject. Before leaving he extracted a promise from the group to take him out hunting the following weekend.

Meanwhile he outfitted himself completely with bow, arrows, special clothing, and all the gadgets and accoutrements related to hunting that he could possibly think of.

The weekend passed without his firing a shot. However, he did see deer, learned a bit about the hunting area, and generally had a great time. By the following weekend he was not only ready to resume the hunt but took on the role of guide. He outfitted a friend and imparted to him his store of newfound woods and bowhunting lore.

Upon arriving at the hunting area the "experienced" novice placed his friend in a blind with some last-minute instructions, then continued on to another blind, which he occupied during the early morning hours. Later, checking back with the first hunter, he was surprised to hear his friend excitedly report a shot at a monstrous buck and a "certain" hit.

They lost no time in starting a search, and although they could not find a blood trail or other evidence, the amateur was so sure he had hit the buck that they kept looking in ever widening circles. After a couple of hours they stumbled upon a great buck, quite dead, and the hunter declared it to be the very one he had shot!

The animal had to be field dressed. Neither man had ever done this or seen it done, but on the strength of office discussion previously overheard, the week-old hunter instructed the day-old hunter in the process.

It proved to be somewhat of a trial . . . but the task was finally accomplished, and the pair of now "old and experienced" hunters proudly transported the animal to a checkpoint for examination and tagging by conservation officers.

"What should I do with it now?" the lucky hunter asked the officer in charge. After another glance and another sniff at the buck, the officer replied, "Well, since this deer was killed with buckshot, I'd say about a week ago, I'd suggest you take him out and bury him!"

BOWHUNTING SEASONS

Some states allow the use of archery tackle during their regular firearms seasons, but hunting under such conditions today is often dangerous. It is necessary to keep under cover as much as possible when bowhunting and to wear cam-

A 4-ton African bull elephant. Brought down by the author, Fred Bear, with a single arrow from a 75-pound bow.

More and more bowhunters are using the compound bow and a bowsight for trophies like this one.

ouflage or other inconspicuous clothing, as the bowman has to get much closer to game than does the rifleman in order to get an effective shot.

Hunting in clothing that blends with the background is not conducive to safety. Fortunately, as all of our states now have either special bowhunting seasons, special bowhunting areas, or both, the archer can get in all the hunting he wants without having to worry about himself becoming the hunted.

State game commissions and firearms hunters have no cause to worry about excessive killing of game by archers. The percentage of game bagged is normally about five deer for every hundred bowhunters. At such a rate, 1,000 archers kill less than 50 deer annually, and 50,000 bowmen will account for about 2,500 deer. It follows that this form of hunting gives as much fun without being as hard on the game populations. Consequently, it is truly a form of conservation.

Deer, like any other species of wildlife, are managed as a renewable natural resource. They may be considered a crop of the land, and, like any other crop, they must be properly harvested

Successful bowhunter, Bill Ellis, packing out the antlers and cape of a large Colorado elk.

each year. Due to ever-increasing industrial and agricultural encroachment on the deer ranges of our country, it has become essential that existing deer herds be held within the capabilities of their habitat to support them. It is far better to harvest surplus animals in legal hunting seasons than to let them die miserably in the deep snows of winter when food becomes critical. It is interesting to note that in such states as Michigan and Wisconsin far more deer die annually of starvation and more perish by highway traffic than are shot by bowhunters.

In the future, as the game areas become even more congested with hunters, bowhunting should prove to be increasingly popular with those who are interested more in the lure of the outdoors than in hunting for meat alone. The true enjoyment of the chase lies in the challenge, the lore, and the battle of wits against instinct—rather than in the full freezer. It is communing with nature, the chief rewards being a refreshed body and a contented soul. A bowhunting license is a permit to use, not abuse, the privileges it entails. It is appreciating our game, respecting fellow hunters and landowners, and giving serious thought to tomorrow.

All state and provincial hunting seasons and bag limits are subject to change each year. Often such changes are not made until shortly before the opening of the hunting season. At the end of this volume is a complete listing of addresses from which you can obtain up-to-date information on seasons, regulations, and license fees.

Chapter XI

UNDERWATER BOWHUNTING

Bowfishing for rough fish is another fine activity open to the owner of archery equipment. In the past ten or twelve years this fast-growing sport has gained thousands of enthusiasts who find it a new source of excitement when the regular game seasons are closed. Nonhunting archers also enjoy it as an interesting variation from target and field shooting.

For most archers, big-game hunting actually occupies a very small part of the year. Unless a bowman can travel from state to state, about the best he can expect in the area of big game is one or two hits a year. The small-game hunter, on the other hand, has something to hunt every day in the year. Rough fish are classified as small game, and available species are to be found almost everywhere in the country. In fresh water some of the most common species hunted are carp, suckers, buffalo, squawfish, dogfish, and gar, while those who live near salt water have innumerable small food species available as well as sting rays, skates, barracuda, and small sharks.

Bowfishing is not only easy and exciting but inexpensive as well. You can obtain a top-quality bowfishing outfit for about $10—not counting a bow, of course. Such an outfit consists of a special reel filled with strong line, a weighted arrow and a harpoon-type point. Some bowfishing reels tape to the back of the bow, and some have a special bracket by which they can be instantly attached or detached from the bow. The reel operates much like a stationary spinning reel and has a small catch built into the edge to keep the nylon fishline from peeling off too soon when making close shots at a sharp downward angle.

Fish weighing 5 pounds or more often roll when hit and can easily break off wood or hollow glass shafts. For this reason bowfishing arrows are made of solid fiber glass. It takes a hearty fish to break one of these shafts. Another advantage of the solid glass arrow is its weight, which makes it possible to shoot accurately through 10 to 15 feet of water. These arrows are usually equipped with rubber or plastic fletching, which saves the archer valuable time formerly spent in straightening out matted feathers.

The barbed harpoon head is usually not fastened permanently to the arrow. The line from the reel is threaded through a small hole in the arrow shaft just ahead of the nock, run down to the forward end of the arrow, and tied through another hole in the head. This puts the drag of the line on the back end of the arrow so that when a hit is made the loosely fitting point with line attached stays in the fish, while the shaft is towed along behind.

When shooting large fish, such as sharks or alligator gar, from a boat, in either fresh or salt water, it is sometimes good sport to bypass the bow reel. Take a fishing rod of the type ordinarily used for the fish to be caught. Pull 15 or 20 yards of line out through the rod guides and coil it carefully in a bucket or on the bottom of the boat. Attach the end of the line to the harpoon arrow. Then, when a hit is made, the bow is laid aside, the rod is quickly picked up, and the

A bowfishing rig in use. Inset shows attachment of reel to bow. (Stedman Studio.)

fish is played as if it were hooked in the mouth.

Where can you go to bowfish? You'll probably find hot fishing spots quite close to your home—the local ponds, streams, bayous, backwaters, lagoons, irrigation canals, and bays that perhaps had nothing to offer when you fished in the usual manner. Many such waters, not containing game fish, harbor a host of rough-and-ready giants just waiting to be taken. An important aspect of this sport is that the taking of such trash fish is a real aid in the conservation of "respectable" game fish—as well as a lot of fun for the bowfisherman.

Perhaps the species that furnish the most sport for the inland archer are the ubiquitous carp and suckers which are found throughout the states. In the first warm days of spring and early summer these fish make their spawning runs into shallow marshes and up small streams. Plenty of action awaits the archer who is on the spot when the carp or suckers are at the peak of their spawning. For best success with these fish, shooting should be done in the middle of the day when the sun is high. The fish are nearer the surface during these

hours. Also, they cannot see the bowfisher as well with the sun silvering the surface of the water. Wearing Polaroid sunglasses will help the bowfisherman, especially when there is a breeze rippling the water, since the specially treated lenses eliminate this surface glare.

Bowfishing can be done from almost any type of boat, but wading is also productive. When wading on a fairly calm day you can see clearly about 30 feet around you.

The arrow must be aimed low to allow for refraction of light in the waters—often a foot underneath the fish being shot at. This compensating factor varies with the angle of the shot. A little experience with a few missed shots is the best way to gain proper judgment of this factor.

Throughout most of the South, and in many other states, the most exciting prey a bowfisherman can stalk are those Pleistocene holdovers, the gars. The glassy-eyed garfish is an ugly, ill-tempered brute with a hide harder than his reputation. A hot sultry day when the sun has warmed the water and garfish are floating just below the surface like a fleet of submarines makes a setting for action that's fast and furious. In many areas gar can be pursued throughout the spring and summer months, along with other rough fish inhabiting the same water, such as buffalo and carp.

There are three types of gar: the longnose, shortnose, and alligator. The first two types are often called "spikebill" or "scissorbill" gars in the South. The shortnose gar seldom exceeds 3 feet in length, while the longnose often grows to more than 5 feet. The alligator gar tops them all, however, often reaching 8 feet in length and weighing over 300 pounds. Six-foot, 100-pound gar are quite common in some waters. The archer who ties into one of these is apt to be quite busy for a spell. It is not too rare for a careless shooter to be yanked overboard following the sudden surge of a torpedoed gar.

Warm summer nights are the best times to hunt the larger gar. A boat and a strong light are needed. Good light is provided by a gasoline lantern with a shield on one side to direct the light away from the shooter. An automobile headlight or a floodlight rigged to a battery works well also. The brighter the light the better.

The best method is for two men to work as a team, one handling the boat while the other

Salt-water bowfishing is excellent sport because of the variety and number of fish which can be taken.

Stalking carp in shallow bays and marshes is an action-packed springtime sport.

The result of a successful stalk and shot. This carp weighs about 20 pounds but they are often found much larger.

Business end of a gar. Note armorlike scale plating and wicked teeth.

shoots, etc. It is a good idea to use a wire fish leader between the harpoon head and line. When bringing a gar into the boat be very careful of his powerful teeth. A hand gaff is very useful. The line should be at least 50-pound test; for the big alligator gar 90-pound test is even better. A few broadhead arrows are handy also on such an excursion for administering a *coup de grâce*.

Salt-water species such as skates and rays are best hunted by cruising slowly over reefs and flats where these "water bats" are feeding on mollusks and other shellfish. The best time is when the tide is ebbing. With caution, the boat can often be brought to within a few feet of the quarry.

Offering excellent shots to an archer standing in the bow of a boat, these fish are extremely powerful for their size. When harpooned, a sting ray measuring 2 or 3 feet across the "wings" can tow a 16-foot boat with ease. An extra 50 to 100 feet of line on your reel is a necessity for this kind of shooting. Again, it is fun to hook up with a fishing rod and play these fish after the harpoon has found its mark. When boating sting rays, be careful of the barbed spine near the base of the tail, and if you should get hold of a barracuda, remember that it has an even bigger mouthful of teeth than the gar.

Most states now have legal seasons for shooting rough fish with the bow; in fact, some offer a year-round open season. A regular fishing license is usually required. In some areas night fishing is legal only with special permission from the Conservation or Fish & Game Department. Be sure to check the fishing laws of your state before going out.

Remember, too, that many so-called rough fish are excellent table fare. Suckers and carp from clean waters are very tasty filleted and smoked. Fish not suitable for eating make excellent fertilizer for flower or vegetable plots.

Harpoon-type arrows can also be used on other game such as bullfrogs, and in this case on alligator. (*Wing Archery Photo.*)

The large leopard ray of the Gulf Stream put up a tremendous battle when harpooned by the bowfisherman.

Chapter XII

NATIONAL ARCHERY ORGANIZATIONS AND THEIR ACTIVITIES

NATIONAL ARCHERY ASSOCIATION

The National Archery Association is the oldest national archery organization in the United States. In the year 1879 the Chicago Archery Association issued a call to all existing archery societies to hold a meeting in Crawfordsville, Indiana, for the purpose of creating a national organization. The meeting was held on January 23 of that year in the office of the Mayor and was attended by representatives of clubs and societies from eight cities. The National Archery Association was established with the famous archer and author Maurice Thompson as its first president. The first Grand National Target Tournament, with 89 participants, was held at Chicago in August of that same year.

Since that date the organization has continued to grow slowly but steadily. In addition to the national target championships, the N.A.A. engages in many other phases of the sport. It provides the rules and background information for local and club competition and state tournaments throughout the United States. It conducts the qualifying U.S. tryouts for the international F.I.T.A. team selections. It is a member of the U. S. Olympic Association, sponsors a Junior Olympic Archery Program, International Mail Tournaments, Interscholastic Mail Tournaments, and Collegiate Mail Tournaments.

Although a dues-paying and therefore allied voting member of the A.A.U., the National Archery Association is the recognized governing body of archery in the United States. It is this country's representative to the international governing body of archery, the F.I.T.A., which it joined in 1932. Individual memberships number about 2,400, but more than 150,000 people target-shoot in competition. The organization helped spearhead the drive to include archery as a sport in the Olympic Games. This goal was realized late in 1965 when the International Archery Association Olympic Committee met in Madrid and voted to include archery as an official Olympic sport, starting with the 1972 Olympic Games. The N.A.A. has charge of conducting qualifications for the U. S. Olympic teams.

In 1974 an annual Field Championship of the Americas was begun under N.A.A. direction. It includes all F.I.T.A. members of North, Central, and South America and islands of the Western Hemisphere.

Membership in the National Archery Association is available on an individual basis for $8 per year, with each additional family member paying $2 per year. Individual memberships for youths under eighteen cost $5 per year.

The present address of the N.A.A. headquarters is 1951 Geraldson Drive, Lancaster, Pennsylvania 17601.

NATIONAL FIELD ARCHERY ASSOCIATION

Although some sort of field shooting had been previously practiced as a novelty or for variety by target archers in Michigan, Wisconsin, Ohio, Oregon, California, and a few other states, this

Professional Archers Association instructor Jack Witt giving class instruction to a group of physical education teachers. (B. Pearson Photo.)

branch of the sport rose to national prominence in California.

In 1934 a group of confirmed bowhunters in Redlands, California, decided that target archery was too formalized for the type of practice they needed and so they constructed the first permanent "field course." Other bowhunting clubs in California soon followed suit. Each club laid out a course to please its own members; consequently, there was a great deal of variance in number of targets, distances shot, etc. The common ground was instinctive shooting style and unknown shooting distances for best bowhunting preparation.

Gradually, through correspondence with bowhunting clubs in other states, enough people of similar mind on the subject were brought together to form a national organization on a temporary basis. This was in 1939, and that year five state organizations plus individual members from eleven other states made up a loosely knit group. That same year Michigan first used the new "standard field round" in its State Championship Tournament.

In 1940 the temporary organization became a permanent one through adoption of a constitution and election of officers. In 1946 the first National Field Tournament was held in Allegan,

Michigan. At that time the membership numbered 4,500. Within seven years the membership had increased to more than 10,000. In the ensuing years considerable changes have been brought about. Today the N.F.A.A. is the largest archery organization in existence, with some 35,000 members on its rolls.

In addition to holding annual National Field Championships, the N.F.A.A. sponsors both indoor and outdoor mail tournaments, awards prizes to members for the taking of large and small game, promotes a variety of archery field games, conducts a continuous public-education program, and works with the various conservation departments through its state associations to bring about favorable bowhunting and conservation legislation.

Membership in the N.F.A.A. is available on an individual basis for $10 per year. Additional memberships within a family are $2 per year. Address of the N.F.A.A. headquarters is Route 1, Box 514, Redlands, California 92373.

FÉDÉRATION INTERNATIONALE de TIR à L'Arc

This organization, the international governing body of archery, was founded in 1931. Thirty-six nations are now members, all of whom classify archery as a national sport. However, only four of these countries in the Western Hemisphere, aside from the United States, are affiliated through national associations. They are Venezuela, Cuba, Mexico, and Canada.

The administrative council of F.I.T.A. has twelve members, representing Belgium, Finland, Czechoslovakia, Great Britain, Poland, Norway, Sweden, East Germany, South Africa, New Zealand, Holland, and the United States. The organization permits each member association to organize ten tournaments at which top scores are entered in competition to establish all-time world archery records. Persons participating in such tournaments in this country must be N.A.A. members and willing to abide by the shooting rules of the International Archery Federation.

The first international tournament was held in the summer of 1931 in Lwow, Poland, with France and Sweden as the only other countries represented. In 1933 the F.I.T.A. moved to London and from that date has been considered a world championship event. Since that time, except for the 1940–46 war years, F.I.T.A. has held international tournaments every year or two, in which special awards are made to the top male and female archers and also to the highest scoring ladies' and gentlemen's teams. There are no major differences between N.A.A. and F.I.T.A. shooting rules.

Since 1957, the first year in which the N.A.A. entered a full team, the United States has dominated international competition. At the present time that dominance is ascribed to the excellent equipment developed in this country, the broad base of participation, and intense competition. Nevertheless, recent scores of other nations indicate that our succeeding performances will have to be improved if the United States is to maintain its number-one position. Japan, Finland, East Germany, France, Italy, Sweden, and Russia are among those countries which are improving rapidly and can be expected to challenge the United States in future tournaments.

The twenty-fourth World Championships took place at Amersfoort, Holland, in 1967; two years later the twenty-fifth Championships were held for the first time in the United States, at Valley Forge, Pennsylvania.

In 1972 the F.I.T.A. Championships coincided with the twentieth Olympiad in Munich, Germany, where the United States won both the men's and women's gold medals. In 1975, Interlaken, Switzerland, was the setting for the World Championships, and in 1976, they again crossed the Atlantic, this time to the Olympic Games held in Montreal, Canada. Once again, U.S. archers took gold medals in both the men's and women's divisions.

F.I.T.A. also holds International Field Archery Championships patterned after the N.F.A.A. rules, but with differences in distances and scoring.

Present headquarters of F.I.T.A. are at 46 The Balk, Walton, Wakefield, England. The United States member of their administrative council is Mr. Clayton Shenk, 1951 Geraldson Drive, Lancaster, Pennsylvania 17601.

PROFESSIONAL ARCHERS ASSOCIATION

The P.A.A. is an organization composed of skilled archers who shoot for prize money and who use their skill to teach archery. Many experienced archery instructors were formerly scattered about the country with no formalized progress or standardized teaching procedures. They recognized the need for leadership and created an organization that would bring them in contact with each other and give direction to the instructional phase of archery.

The P.A.A. was firmly established in 1963 when it held the first National P.A.A. Tournament in Daytona Beach, Florida. Its stated objectives are: to elevate the standard of the professional archer's vocation, to promote interest in the sport of archery, to protect the mutual interests of all its members, to assist deserving members who may be out of employment to obtain a position, and any other similar objectives which may arise.

The P.A.A. Instruction Committee provides an in-service training program designed to bring the latest methods of teaching to its members. In order to become a member in the capacity of an official instructor, an applicant must be eighteen years of age or over, must pass a written examination, and must meet other requirements as set forth by the P.A.A. Constitution. Members must appear before a reviewing board every three years for recertification.

The current address of P.A.A. headquarters is c/o Joyce Otter, Executive Secretary, 5430 South Brennan Road, Hemlock, Michigan 48626.

AMERICAN INDOOR ARCHERY ASSOCIATION

The A.I.A.A. is made up of members with many years of experience in all phases of archery who, with the cooperation of league members and operators of modern indoor-archery facilities, have embarked upon a program to insure the greatest amount of competition, satisfaction, and enjoyment from participation in archery games.

The A.I.A.A. has developed a number of games, target faces, and scoring methods to meet the needs of present and future indoor-archery establishments, as well as of archery clubs that shoot in indoor leagues. One of its key goals is standardization of indoor rounds and rules to avoid confusion between various regions, and to adopt scoring systems that will be understandable to all types of news media and to spectators.

Some fifteen basic rounds or games designed for league play and tournament competition are presently sanctioned by the A.I.A.A. as well as a number of novelty events to add to the appeal of indoor archery for family and club participation. In connection with the specialized rounds, target faces have been developed to provide the best possible visibility for both players and spectators, and to facilitate scoring systems in team handicapping.

The A.I.A.A. has published a wealth of excellent literature concerning recommended procedures for forming and managing teams and leagues, correct nomenclature for these activities, rules for shooting-line courtesy, scoring sheets, suggested awards and eligibility rules for same, and safety and maintenance requirements for lanes certification.

Detailed information concerning membership can be obtained by addressing inquiries to A.I.A.A., P. O. Box 925, Gainesville, Florida 32601.

AMERICAN ARCHERY COUNCIL

The American Archery Council encompasses all sections of archery and includes in its membership the American Indoor Archery Association, the Archery Lane Operators Association, National Archery Association, National Field Archery Association, Archery Manufacturers Association, Pope and Young Club, Professional Bowhunters Society, Professional Archers Association, Bowhunters Who Care, Fred Bear Sports Club, and the Archery Hall of Fame.

The Council concerns itself primarily with public relations designed to aid the growth of archery in all its phases. As the voice of archery, it functions through a number of committees.

Additional information can be obtained from the headquarters at 200 Castlewood Road, North Palm Beach, Florida 33408.

FRED BEAR SPORTS CLUB

The Fred Bear Sports Club (F.B.S.C.) is an action-oriented organization dedicated to the welfare of our ecology, proper wildlife management, and the preservation of our hunting heritage. The Club was founded in 1972 at Grayling, Michigan. Cofounder and executive director is Dick Lattimer, with Fred Bear as honorary director.

Since that time it has enrolled more than 25,000 members, worldwide, in its cause. F.B.S.C. has spent over $500,000 on special projects to help preserve hunting rights and aid scientific wildlife management. It has its own publication, *The Big Sky,* as well as an achievement awards system for both indoor shooting and legally taken game, and is very active on the national level in fulfilling its commitments.

Membership fee in the F.B.S.C. is $5. Present headquarters are at Fred Bear Drive and Archer Road, Gainesville, Florida 32601.

NATIONAL CROSSBOW ORGANIZATIONS

The late H. L. Bailey was the person most responsible for the long campaign to win recognition for the crossbow as a competitive-archery implement in this country. Mr. Bailey became interested in the crossbow after seeing movies showing its use, and, as far as is known, he developed the first modern target crossbow in the United States. Although Mr. Bailey interested other archers in his revised device, the N.A.A. remained adamant in its regulation, which stated: "Any bow—except a crossbow—may be used in any event in recognized competition."

A few of the Pope and Young Club World Record Bowhunting trophies on display.

Finally, in 1947, the N.A.A. relented and admitted a crossbow division to their National Championships. Although the number of crossbow enthusiasts is nowhere near that of longbow archers, the crossbowmen ranks are gradually increasing as more people become familiar with this sport. It is at present almost entirely a target sport. Because the crossbow is classed as a mechanical arm, its use in archery-hunting seasons is banned by most states, and in only four or five places is it presently a legal hunting weapon.

There are three major crossbow associations, each composed chiefly of regional groups. The National Crossbowmen of the United States is a division of the National Archery Association. Crossbow archers shoot in N.A.A. tournaments but never compete against archers using regular bows. The majority of those competing at the N.A.A. National are members of the National Crossbowmen. Information on the activities of the National Crossbowmen can be obtained by writing Mr. Gilbert Frey, 203 Laytonville Road,

Washington Grove, Maryland 20880.

The other two associations are the American Crossbow Association, c/o George Stevens, P. O. Box 72, Huntsville, Arkansas 72740; and the National Crossbow Hunters Association, c/o Jack Bowman, 1010 Concord Avenue, Piqua, Ohio 45356. The members of these two organizations have their own tournament schedules.

Because of lack of information for the general public, there is not as yet a large market for crossbows in this country. The majority are either custom made by a few individuals or made by the shooters themselves. Sources of custom-made crossbows, as well as plans for making these weapons, are available from both the National Crossbowmen and the National Company of Crossbowmen.

THE POPE AND YOUNG CLUB®

The Pope and Young Club is a scientific organization dedicated to promoting conservation and high ethical standards in bowhunting, and serves as a recognized repository for official bowhunting records of North American big-game animals. It had its beginnings in 1957 when a few dedicated bowmen decided to provide their sport with a system of records and awards patterned after the world-famous Boone and Crockett Club of New York. They chose to name the club in honor of the two renowned bowhunters, Dr. Saxton Pope and Arthur Young, who did so much to popularize this sport in America.

The first organizational meeting and presentation of awards for world-record big-game trophies was held during the 1960 N.F.A.A. Championships in Grayling, Michigan.

On June 5, 1963, the Club was fully incorporated in the State of Washington as a scientific, nonprofit organization.

The Pope and Young Club provides that at no time shall there be more than 100 Regular Members, and a limited number of Associate Members. Regular Members must have taken with bow and arrow, under rules of fair chase, three different species of North American big-game animals, at least one of which shall be in the trophy class meeting the minimum scoring-point requirements for listing in the Club's records repository. In addition to the above membership classifications, there is a new one called Senior Member. In order to qualify, Senior Members must have taken with bow and arrow, under the Club's rules of fair chase, at least one adult animal of each of four of the various species of North American big game, of which three will be in the trophy class meeting or exceeding the minimum scoring-point requirements for listing in the Club's records repository. Applicant must have been a Regular Member for at least five years.

A roster of Official Measurers, maintained throughout the country, score trophies for registration in the biennial competitions. The data secured from the skulls, tusks, horns, and antlers submitted go into the archives as part of the file of records of North American big game. To date, there are upwards of 2,000 record-class trophies in their files.

The Pope and Young competitions are open to anyone. One does not have to be a member to submit a trophy for recognition. Animals must be taken with bow and arrow under the Rules of Fair Chase during legal hunting seasons. Bowhunters are thus encouraged toward more qualitative hunting by awakening interest in outstanding examples of trophy game animals on this continent. This organization is recognized throughout the sporting world as the authority on such trophies taken with the bow and arrow.

The current address of the Pope and Young Club® is c/o Naomi J. Torrey, Executive Secretary, Route 1, Box 147, Salmon, Idaho 83467.

Following are the latest bowhunting world records of North American big game as listed by the Pope and Young Club at the close of the 11th recording period on December 31, 1978.

POPE AND YOUNG CLUB® WORLD RECORDS OF NORTH
AMERICAN ANTLERED AND HORNED GAME ANIMALS

SPECIES AND MINIMUM SCORE FOR ENTRY		WHERE TAKEN	BOWHUNTER	WORLD RECORD SCORE	
*† Whitetail deer (typical antlers)	125	Illinois	Mel J. Johnson	204 4/8	1965
*† Whitetail deer (nontypical antlers)	150	Nebraska	Del Austin	279 7/8	1962
Mule deer (typical antlers)	145	Colorado	Ronald E. Sniff	197	1969
Mule deer (nontypical antlers)	160	Colorado	Dean Derby II	246 6/8	1976
† Blacktail deer	90	Oregon	B. G. Shurtleff	172 2/8	1969
Coues deer	68	Arizona	Larry Peterson	104 2/8	1978
† Alaska-Yukon moose	170	Alaska	Dr. Michael Cusack	248	1973
Canada moose	135	British Columbia	Peter Halbig	201 4/8	1968
Wyoming (Shiras) moose	115	Montana	Keith Wheat	159 1/8	1960
Alaska brown bear (Kodiak bear)	20	Alaska	Fred Bear	28	1960
Polar bear	20	Alaska	Richard McIntyre	26 6/8	1958
Grizzly bear	19	British Columbia	Harley Tison	25 6/16	1972
Black bear	18	Saskatchewan	Ray Mastel (tie)	21 11/16	1974
		Idaho	Harold Boyack	21 11/16	1976
† Barren Ground caribou	300	Alaska	Art Kragness	446 6/8	1970
Mountain caribou	265	British Columbia	Melvin K. Wolf	390 1/8	1970
Woodland caribou	220	Newfoundland	Dempsey Cape	345 2/8	1966
Rocky Mountain goat	40	Washington	Bob Haugen	50	1971
† Bighorn sheep	130	Colorado	Doy Curtis	179 3/8	1977
Stone sheep	120	British Columbia	Fred Bear	158 1/8	1957
Dall sheep	120	Alaska	Robert Hansen	163 1/8	1971
Desert bighorn sheep	115	No entry submitted in this category as yet.			
Roosevelt elk	210	Washington	Jess Martin, Jr.	293 5/8	1971
Yellowstone elk	240	Arizona	Doug Kittredge	380 2/8	1975
Pronghorn antelope	57	North Dakota	Archie Malm	85	1958
Cougar	13	Idaho	Doug Kittredge	15 8/16	1971
Jaguar	14	Mexico	Bill Mastrangel	14 7/16	1959
Bison	80	Alaska	George Moerlein	112 2/8	1972
Muskox	65	Alaska	Joseph Fogleman	106 4/8	1976

* These two magnificent whitetail-deer records are also recognized by the Boone and Crockett Club as the top trophy (typical) and second place (nontypical) trophy in existence for which the hunter and circumstances of kill are known. Mel Johnson's trophy won the Sagamore Hill Award, the highest honor given by the Boone and Crockett Club and one of only twelve such awards given in their history.

Many of the other bowhunting trophies in the Pope and Young Club records are also recognized and listed by the Boone and Crockett Club in their world records of game taken by any means.

For further information on the Pope and Young Club and its activities, write to Naomi Torrey, Executive Secretary, Route 1, Box 147, Salmon, Idaho 83467.

† Pope and Young Club Ishi Award winners. Early in 1964, the Executive Committee of the Pope and Young Club initiated a special bowhunting trophy, intended as an equivalent to Boone and Crockett's Sagamore Hill Award, established in honor of Theodore Roosevelt. This award of highest recognition was named the Pope and Young Club's Ishi Award, in honor of the last of the Yana Indians and the bowhunting teacher of Dr. Saxton Pope and Arthur Young. The Ishi trophies are not given at any designated intervals, but only when a truly magnificent and outstanding big game trophy is recorded.

The Ishi Award was designed for the most part by Fred Bear. It features a specially made obsidian spear point, hand-chipped by Jim Ramsey of Lincoln, New Mexico, who is perhaps the finest living exponent of this ancient Indian art. The background of the award is an oval plaque of Brazilian rosewood on which the Pope and Young Club medallion (face and back) is inset, along with a silver engraving plate.

The first recipient of an Ishi Award was Del Austin for his tremendous nontypical whitetail deer. Mel Johnson's record-setting typical whitetail received the second Ishi Award. A third Award was given to Doy Curtis for his bighorn sheep. A fourth went to Art Kragness for a great Barren Ground caribou, a fifth for Dr. Michael Cusack's record Alaska-Yukon moose, and the sixth, and latest, was given for B. G. Shurtleff's world record blacktail deer.

Whitetail Deer (Typical)
Score: 204 4/8
Locality: Peoria County, Illinois
Hunter: Melvin J. Johnson

Whitetail Deer (Non-Typical)
Score: 279 7/8
Locality: Shelton, Nebraska
Hunter: Del Austin

Mule Deer (Typical)
Score: 197
Locality: Guffy, Colorado
Hunter: Ronald E. Sniff

Mule Deer (*Non-Typical*)
Score: 236 1/8
Locality: Kaibab Forest, Arizona
Hunter: Stanley McIntyre

Blacktail Deer
Score: 160 7/8
Locality: Jackson County, Oregon
Hunter: Dr. G. Scott Jennings

Coues Deer
Score: 100 6/8
Locality: Graham Mountain, Arizona
Hunter: Hugh H. Hamman

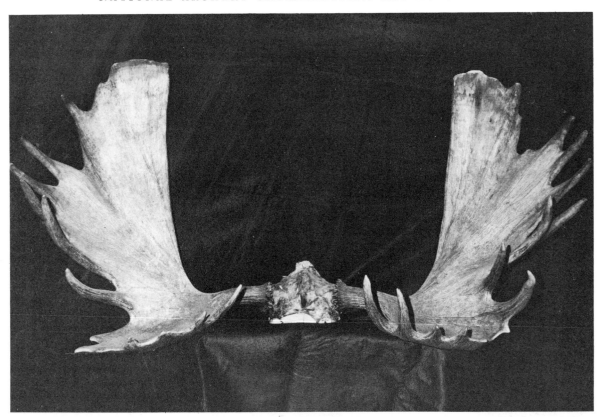

Alaskan-Yukon Moose
Score: 248
Locality: Alaska Peninsula
Hunter: Michael Cusack, M.D.

Canada Moose
Score: 201 4/8
Locality: Mt. Lady Lourier, B.C., Canada
Hunter: Peter Halbig

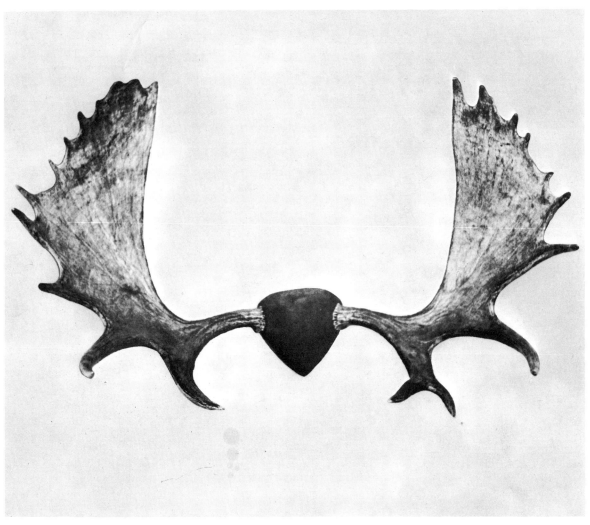

Wyoming Moose
Score: 159 1/8
Locality: Gallatin County, Montana
Hunter: Keith Wheat

Barren Ground Caribou
Score: 446 6/8
Locality: Alaska Peninsula
Hunter: Art Kragness

Mountain Caribou
Score: 390 1/8
Locality: Firesteel Lake, Canada
Hunter: Melvin K. Wolf

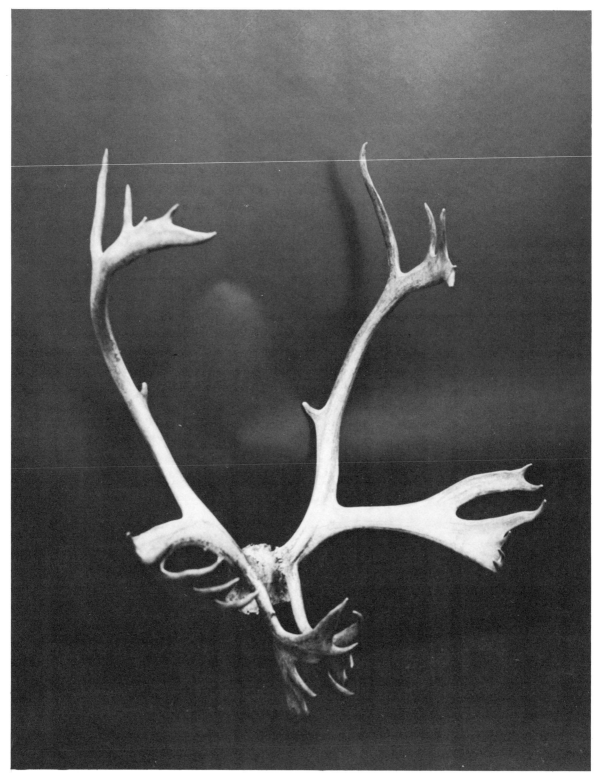

Woodland Caribou
Score: 345 2/8
Locality: Victoria River, Canada
Hunter: Dempsey Cape

Rocky Mountain Goat
Score: 50
Locality: Kittitas County, Washington
Hunter: Bob Haugen

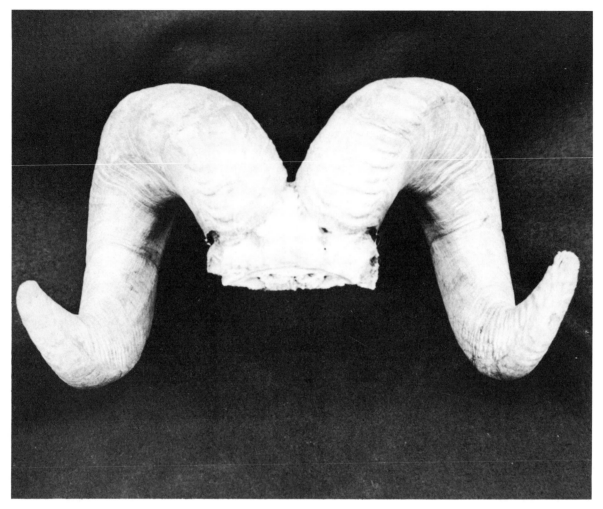

Bighorn Sheep
Score: 176 3/8
Locality: Sweet Grass Area, Montana
Hunter: Ray Alt

Stone Sheep
Score: 158 1/8
Locality: Cassiar District, Canada
Hunter: Fred Bear

Dall Sheep
Score: 163 1/8
Locality: Chugach Mountains, Alaska
Hunter: Robert C. Hansen

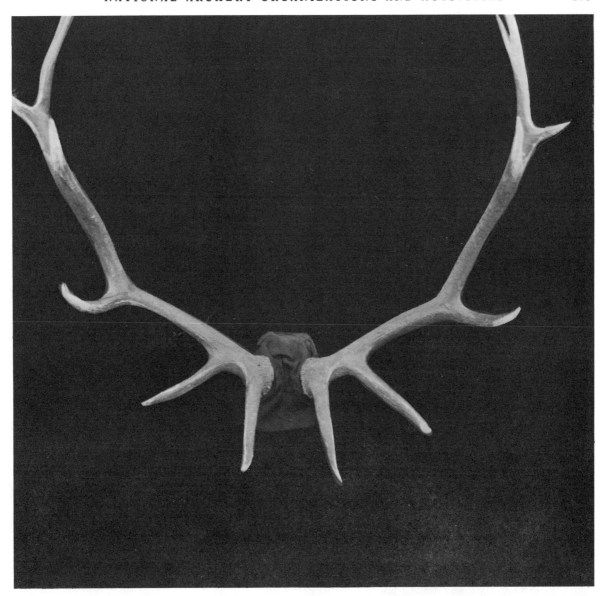

Roosevelt Elk
Score: 293 5/8
Locality: Long Island, Washington
Hunter: Jess Martin, Jr.

Yellowstone Elk
Score: 380 2/8
Locality: San Francisco Peaks, Arizona
Hunter: Doug Kittredge

Pronghorn Antelope
Score: 85
Locality: Raleigh, North Dakota
Hunter: Archie Malm

Muskox
Score: 106 4/8
Locality: Nunivak Island, Alaska
Hunter: Joseph Fogleman

Woodland Caribou
Score: 345 2/8
Locality: Victorian River, Canada
Hunter: Dempsey Cape

Chapter XIII

ARCHERY SAFETY AND EQUIPMENT CARE

No bow and arrow is a toy. Many persons fail to realize that the danger of injury from an arrow is always present. Even the blunt rubber tips on "dime-store sets" can put out an eye if shot at close range. And any of the metal tips used in target archery can be lethal even if shot from a lightweight bow.

Before placing archery tackle in the hands of a youngster, you must be sure that he is aware of basic safety principles. As with firearms, proper pretraining will help prevent later disaster. The primary rule of course is: "Never point an arrow at anyone or anything you do not want to shoot." Songbirds, chipmunks, squirrels, and every other living creature must be placed in the "off limits" category. Teaching youngsters sport without sportsmanship is irresponsible.

Children should never be allowed to shoot except under adult supervision, and during all training respect for safety should be foremost. Shooting arrows up in the air, failure to make sure the target area is clear, or pointing a nocked arrow in any direction but at the target should not be allowed.

TARGET SAFETY

Anything worth doing at all is worth doing right. This maxim applies to archery target shooting as much as to any other sport. Before anyone starts to shoot, an inspection of equipment is essential. As I said earlier, most bow breakage is due to improper stringing and/or mishandling. Therefore, the first consideration in the handling of equipment is learning to string a bow properly. After stringing, be sure the string loops are securely seated in the bow nocks. At the same time check to see that your bowstring is not frayed or worn and that the arrow nocking point has not slipped. Next, check all of the arrows you intend to use. Be sure the fletching is on tight, and in the case of wood or glass arrows, check for cracks and splinters.

Never try out another person's equipment unless expressly invited to do so. Never draw and release a bow without an arrow in it. Such dry-shooting puts a terrific strain on the bow limbs and string and can result in a broken bow. NEVER SHOOT ARROWS STRAIGHT UP TO SEE HOW HIGH THEY WILL GO. An arrow is as dangerous falling as ascending and is harder to see. If you want to watch your arrows soar through the blue, flight-shoot on an open expanse away from people.

Do not use targets that won't stop arrows unless you have a suitable backstop such as a sandbank or a hillside. Remember, too, that arrows can glance off trees or other solid objects and change course. For this reason, you must be sure that not only is your line of flight to the target clear, but that the area behind the target is clear also. If you or one of your party loses an arrow behind a target butt, lean the bows against the face of the target while searching behind it so they can readily be seen from the shooting position.

Always use an arm guard. Just one slap of the bowstring can raise a painful welt on the arm if it

An excellent project for clubs or leagues is a safety teaching program with the aid of slides. The Genessee Conservation League of Rochester, New York, is shown giving such a program, which in the state of New York is compulsory for previously unlicensed bowhunters.

is not protected. When two archers are shooting at the same target, the one who finishes first should step quietly back from the shooting line and wait for the other to finish. If while shooting in competition an arrow falls from your bow in front of you, you may retrieve and shoot it only if you can pull it back with your bow tip without leaving the shooting position.

In target archery an arrow that either rebounds from the scoring face or that passes through the scoring face so that it is not visible from the front can be counted as 7 points at 60 yards or less, and as 5 points for ranges beyond 60 yards if other shooters witnessed the shot. In field archery a bounce-out or pass-through can be counted as 3 points if witnessed by other shooters.

When pulling arrows from a target, always grasp the shaft with both hands close to the target face and pull straight back. This method of withdrawal prevents shafts from bending and prolongs the life of the target face. When drawing an arrow from the ground, don't pull up on it but draw it out at the same angle it entered. Last but not least, no matter how expert you are, never permit anyone to hold a target for you. This risky procedure has turned fun into tragedy. Common sense makes for safe archery.

HUNTING SAFETY

Armor, as worn on the battlefield at the time of the Norman Conquest, was made obsolete by the devastating effect of the English longbow and the broadhead arrow. Such arrows move at less than 200 feet per second but under some conditions will penetrate bulletproof materials. So with regard to safety precautions, the sharp hunting arrow demands the greatest respect.

Perhaps the most important rule for bowhunters is: NO MATTER WHAT METHOD YOU USE TO CARRY EXTRA HUNTING ARROWS AFIELD, ALWAYS KEEP THE BROADHEADS COVERED FOR YOUR OWN PROTECTION AND FOR THE PROTECTION OF THOSE AROUND YOU. Do not carry arrows loose in a car. Keep them in a quiver or a rack to protect the occupants and to maintain the sharpness of the broadheads. Never use a bow quiver or any other type of hunting quiver that does not have a protective hood or covering for the sharpened heads.

When walking alongside or behind companions in the field, do not carry a hunting arrow nocked on the bowstring. You can easily trip or stumble and injure one of them. NOCK A HUNTING

Youngsters beginning in archery should always have adult supervision and be thoroughly schooled in the proper safety rules.

The step-through method is used by bow-hunter Bob Hood to string his hunting bow. (Michigan Tourist Council Photo. #55S 1469.)

ARROW ONLY IN IMMEDIATE ANTICI-
PATION OF A SHOT.

Do not jump a ditch or climb through a fence with an arrow on the string or in the hand. Place your bow and arrow through a fence before climbing over or through. After a fall, check your equipment to see that the bow is not cracked and that no strands of the bowstring are cut.

When using an elevated blind or stand, pull up your bow and quiver with a length of cord after you have climbed to position.

Never be in such a hurry that you neglect the precautions in stringing or unstringing your bow. Either carry a cord-type bowstringer in your pocket and habitually use it or be very careful in using a hand method. This precaution has been mentioned before but is repeated here because bowstringing is one of the most dangerous and neglected phases of archery, and especially so under the excitement of hunting. Each time you string a bow, hold it well away from your face while checking for proper alignment of the bowstring loops in the nocks and over the re-curves.

Check the fistmele occasionally. If it becomes low it may be a sign of separated fibers in the string, possibly under a serving, which could lead to a break at a most inopportune moment. Never shoot a bow with a frayed bowstring. If the string breaks during a shot, the bow may break also. Carry a spare string with you at all times. Also, occasionally check for loose fletching on your arrows.

Be sure of your target and never release an arrow if you are unable to see its full path to the target. Remember that an arrow can be deflected by a branch or twig a considerable distance away from its original course. Never attempt to shoot over the head of a companion.

For any hunting shot, always concentrate on the exact spot on the game you want to hit. This practice will not only greatly increase your chance for a clean kill but will discourage the habit of shooting at undefinable objects in cover.

When bowhunting during a firearms season, it may be wise to forego the use of camouflage clothing.

When wearing bulky clothing in cold weather, always use an arm guard large enough to keep the sleeve out of the way of the bowstring.

Before entering the woods to hunt, tell someone where you are going and when you expect to return. Always carry a strong knife, a supply of waterproof matches, some Band-Aids, candy bars or other snacks, a map of the area you are hunting and a compass. Strangely, many hunters who carry a compass fail to use it properly. All you really need to know is that if you leave a north-south road and head west to hunt, you need only turn east to find the road again. But you have to know that you went west in the first place. This should be checked before starting out, not after you find yourself confused.

In the field the archer's code of conduct is predicated on the necessity of safeguarding himself and his fellow hunters from avoidable and regrettable accidents. Safety and courtesy can be considered synonymous terms in archery. To practice one is to assure the other.

CARE OF EQUIPMENT

When not in use, keep the bow unstrung. To store your bow, hang it vertically by the bowstring or place it across two pegs in a horizontal position. Never leave it standing on end. Always store it in a cool dry place, such as a closet next to an outside wall. Basements and attics are particularly poor storage areas, as they are often too hot, too cold, or too dry.

Make sure your bow is dry before storing. A bowcase lined with soft cloth or sheepskin lends extra protection and helps to keep moisture from the bow. It is beneficial to occasionally give the bow a light coat of furniture or automobile wax to protect the finish from scratches and help keep out moisture. Do not leave your bow in a closed car in hot weather.

Correct bowstrings are most important. Use only the length and weight string recommended by the manufacturer of your bow. A string that is too heavy will make your bow sluggish, while a string that is too light may break, causing breakage of the bow as well. Most new strings, even though prestretched, will stretch again slightly after a little use. The string length can then be adjusted by twisting, but do not twist in the direction opposite to the original twist, as this loosens the servings and weakens the string. The bowstring should be kept well waxed at all times to prevent fraying. Archery dealers sell a special beeswax cake for this purpose.

In attaching accessories such as bowsights,

don't place screws through sections that bend. Tape will do the job just as well.

Arrow fletching that has become matted through exposure to the elements can be brought back to shape by holding it over the steam from a teakettle. When broadhead arrows have been sharpened, the heads should be lightly coated with oil or vaseline to keep them from rusting. Paraffin or furniture wax rubbed on arrow shafts makes them easier to withdraw from bales, and in the case of hunting arrows, aids in penetration. Arrows should be stored in a wall rack, in the carton in which they came, or loosely in quivers. If you pack too many in one quiver, the feathers may become pressed out of shape.

Give your bow and other tackle the same intelligent care you would give to any fine sporting equipment.

This bowhunter is ignoring a cardinal rule by walking around camp with a broadhead arrow nocked. The only time a hunting arrow should be on the string is in immediate preparation for a shot. (Michigan Tourist Council Photo. ⅍55S 1471.)

Over much of our country, bowhunting seasons occur when days and nights in the open are among the finest of the year. This is one of the big reasons so many gun hunters are adding a hunting bow to their arsenal.

"The long delicious trails and mountain paths are yours. The ecstasy of cool running streams I give you freely when athirst. And last of all I leave to you the thrill of life and the joy of youth that throbs a moment in a well-bent bow, then leaps forth in the flight of an arrow." —The Adventurous Bowman *by Dr. Saxton Pope (Stedman Studio.)*

APPENDIX I: DIRECTORY OF BOWHUNTING INFORMATION SOURCES

The following agencies are sources of information on hunting seasons and regulations, license fees, etc.

NOTE: Many states do not set hunting seasons until June or July of the year in which they apply.

THE UNITED STATES

ALABAMA: Alabama Department of Conservation, Fish and Game Division, Montgomery 36100

ALASKA: Department of Fish and Game, Juneau 99801

ARIZONA: Game and Fish Commission, State Building, Phoenix 85000

ARKANSAS: Arkansas Game and Fish Commission, Little Rock 72200

CALIFORNIA: Department of Fish and Game, 722 Capitol Avenue, Sacramento 95801

COLORADO: Game, Fish and Parks Department, 6060 Broadway, Denver 80200

CONNECTICUT: Department of Agriculture and Natural Resources, Board of Fisheries and Game, Hartford 06100

DELAWARE: Board of Game and Fish Commissioners, Dover, 19901

FLORIDA: Game and Fish Commission, Tallahassee 32301

GEORGIA: State Game and Fish Commission, 401 State Capitol, Atlanta 30300

HAWAII: Department of Land and Natural Resources, Division of Fish and Game, Honolulu 96800

IDAHO: Fish and Game Department, 600 South Walnut, Boise 83700

ILLINOIS: Department of Conservation, Springfield 62700

INDIANA: Department of Natural Resources, Division of Fish and Game, Indianapolis 46200

IOWA: State Conservation Commission, East 7th and Court, Des Moines 50300

KANSAS: Forestry, Fish and Game Commission, Pratt 67124

KENTUCKY: Department of Fish and Wildlife Resources, State Office Building, Frankfort 40601

LOUISIANA: Louisiana Wildlife and Fisheries Commission, 400 Royal Street, New Orleans 70100

MAINE: Department of Inland Fisheries and Game, Augusta 04330

MARYLAND: Department of Game and Inland Fish, State Office Building, Annapolis 21400

MICHIGAN: Department of Natural Resources, Lansing 48900

MINNESOTA: Department of Conservation, Division of Fish and Game, St. Paul 55100

MISSISSIPPI: Game and Fish Commission, Box 451, Jackson 39200

MISSOURI: Department of Conservation, Jefferson City 65101

MONTANA: Fish and Game Department, Helena 59601

NEBRASKA: Game, Forestation and Parks Commission, Lincoln 68500

NEVADA: Fish and Game Commission, Reno 89500

NEW HAMPSHIRE: Fish and Game Department, 34 Bridge Street, Concord 03301

NEW JERSEY: Department of Conservation, Division of Fish and Game, Trenton 08600

NEW MEXICO: Department of Fish and Game, Santa Fe 87501

NEW YORK: Conservation Department, Division of Fish and Game, Albany 12200

NORTH CAROLINA: Wildlife Resources Commission, Division of Game, Raleigh 27600

NORTH DAKOTA: Game and Fish Department, Bismarck 58501

OHIO: Department of Natural Resources, Division of Wildlife, Columbus 43200

OKLAHOMA: Department of Wildlife Conservation, State Capitol Building, Oklahoma City 73100

OREGON: State Game Commission, Portland 97200

PENNSYLVANIA: Pennsylvania Game Commission, Harrisburg 17101

RHODE ISLAND: Department of Natural Resources, Providence 02900

SOUTH CAROLINA: Wildlife Resources Department, Division of Game, Columbia 29200

SOUTH DAKOTA: Department of Game, Fish and Parks, Pierre 57501

TENNESSEE: Game and Fish Commission, Nashville 37200

TEXAS: Parks and Wildlife Department, State Office Building, Austin 78700

UTAH: Department of Fish and Game, 1596 W. North Temple, Salt Lake City 48100

VERMONT: Fish and Game Department, Montpelier 05602

VIRGINIA: Commission of Game and Inland Fisheries, Richmond 23200

WASHINGTON: Department of Game, Olympia 98501

WEST VIRGINIA: Department of Natural Resources, Charleston 25300

WISCONSIN: State Conservation Department, Madison 53700

WYOMING: Game and Fish Commission, Box 1589, Cheyenne 82001

CANADIAN PROVINCES

ALBERTA: Department of Lands and Forests, Edmonton

BRITISH COLUMBIA: Fish and Game Branch, Department of Recreation and Conservation, Victoria

MANITOBA: Department of Mines and Natural Resources, Director of Game, Winnipeg

NEW BRUNSWICK: Minister of Lands and Mines, Director of Game, Fredericton

NEWFOUNDLAND: Department of Mines and Resources, Director of Game, St. Johns

NOVA SCOTIA: Department of Lands and Forests, Halifax

ONTARIO: Department of Lands and Forests, Toronto

QUEBEC: Federation of Fish and Game Associations, Montreal

SASKATCHEWAN: Fish and Game League, Saskatoon

YUKON TERRITORY: Director of Game, Box 2703, Whitehorse

APPENDIX II: MAJOR ARCHERY EQUIPMENT MANUFACTURERS

Free descriptive catalogs may be obtained by writing to the following:

American Archery Company
  P. O. Box 100
  Industrial Park, Oconto Falls, Wisconsin 54154

Bear Archery
  Subsidiary of Walter Kidde & Company, Inc.
  Rural Route 4
  4600 Southwest 41st Boulevard
  Gainesville, Florida 32601

Ben Pearson, Inc.
  P. O. Box 7465
  Pine Bluff, Arkansas 71611

Browning Archery
  Morgan, Utah 84050

Darton, Inc.
  3261 Flushing Road
  Flint, Michigan 48504

Damon Howatt Archery, Inc.
  Route 8
  Yakima, Washington 98901

Jas. D. Easton, Inc.
  7800 Haskell Avenue
  Van Nuys, California 91406

Hoyt Archery Company
  11510 Natural Bridge
  Bridgeton, Missouri 63044

Indian Archery Corporation
  16–24 Clark Street
  Evansville, Indiana 47708

Jennings Compound Bows, Inc.
  28756 North Castaic Canyon Road
  Valencia, California 91355

Martin Archery, Inc.
  Route 5, Box 127
  Walla Walla, Washington 99362

Precision Shooting Equipment, Inc.
  Mahomet, Illinois 61853

Saunders Archery Target Company
  Box 476
  Columbus, Nebraska 68601

Wilson Brothers Manufacturing Company
  Route 8, Box 33H
  Springfield, Missouri 65804

Wing Archery (AMF-Voit)
  Santa Ana, California 92704

Woodcraft Equipment Company
  P. O. Box 110
  Independence, Missouri 64051

Yamaha International
  6600 Orangethorpe Avenue
  Buena Park, California 90620

APPENDIX III: A.A.C. ARCHERY RANGES

THE DESIGN

The most important considerations in the design are:

1. Safety—This range is an open-air archery facility constructed in such a way that it can be located in either isolated or high traffic areas. The angle of the side walls and overhead baffles make it impossible for an arrow to leave the range enclosure.

2. Low Construction Cost—This archery range costs about the same to construct as a double tennis court. A tennis court can accommodate four players at a time. This A.A.C. archery range will accommodate eight shooters at a time in individual practice or sixteen archers at a time in organized league shooting.

3. Low Maintenance—Thanks to a unique cantilevered target butt design, developed especially for this A.A.C. range, maintenance is kept to a bare minimum. Corrugated cardboard is used in place of the traditional straw and a weight similar to a window sash, in a ratio of five to one, keeps a constant pressure on the board to compensate for normal arrow penetration wear. The range also features a gravel surface.

4. Maximum Utilization of Space—Space required is just 55 feet by 105 feet. This compares to the 120 feet by 120 feet for a double tennis court. There are eight shooting lanes with targets at 30 meters and 10 meters, in keeping with international competition. The design is esthetically

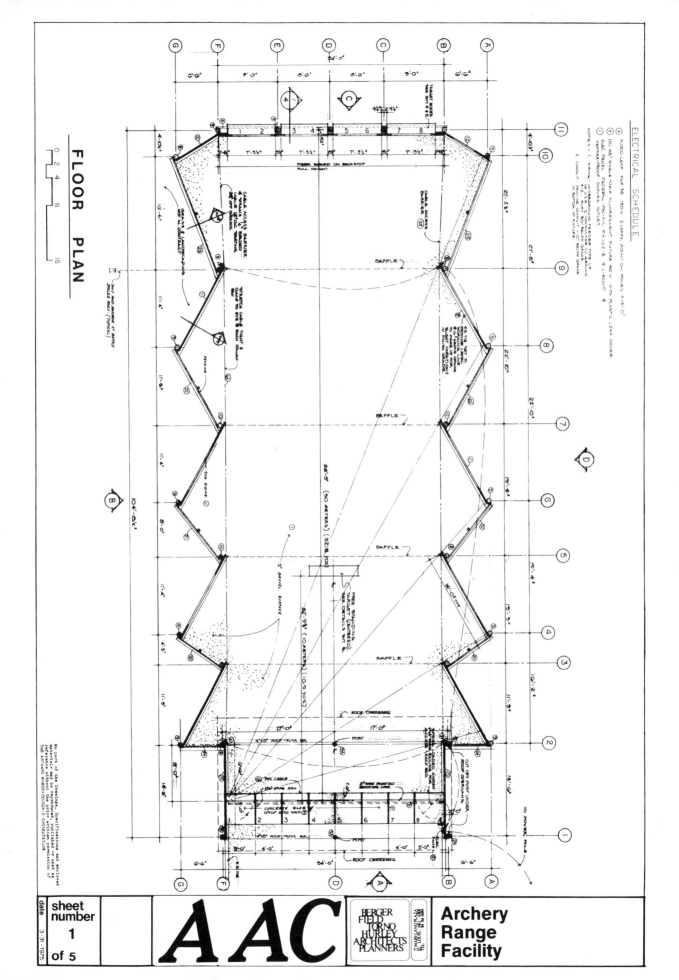

FLOOR PLAN

ELECTRICAL SCHEDULE

BERGER
FIELD
TORNO
HURLEY
ARCHITECTS
PLANNERS

AAC

**Archery
Range
Facility**

date 3-31-1975

sheet number 1 of 5

clean, and the covered interior shooting line contains complete archery self-instruction signs and shooting-etiquette standards. The addition of lights at the shooting line and at the targets can extend the use of the range.

5. Adaptability—The range design is clean and adapts itself well to a wide variety of locations, landscaping, and terrain. It will blend in well with its surroundings.

This American Archery Council range was designed for A.A.C. by Don Ruble of Berger, Torno & Hurley Architects, St. Louis, Missouri.

HOW TO OBTAIN PLANS

A set of architect's blueprints, materials list and building specifications for this A.A.C. range is available from the A.A.C. office at 200 Castlewood Road, North Palm Beach, Florida 33408, at a cost of $10 for the complete package. Extra copies of just the blueprints for your use in obtaining quotations are available for $5 per set. Please enclose check or money order made out to the American Archery Council in the correct amount.

To assist you in any area with your archery program, contact Mr. Mike Schneider, acting executive secretary of A.A.C., at the above address. There is a scale model of this range available for you to use in presenting this idea to your Park Board or other interested group.

HOW TO FINANCE THIS NEW A.A.C. ARCHERY RANGE

Funds for the construction, operation, and maintenance of public target ranges such as this new A.A.C. Range are available through your State Fish & Game Department (Attention: Hunter Safety Coordinator) under public law 91-503 and public law 92-558 which amended the Federal Aid in Wildlife Restoration Act of 1937, the Pittman-Robertson Act (U.S.C. 669-669i; 50 Stat. 917). According to the Department of the Interior "The 11 percent excise tax on bows and arrows collected by the Department of the Treasury shall be apportioned each year through statutory formulae to the State Fish & Game Departments, in proportion to the ratio that the population of each state bears to the population of all states . . . provided that each state shall be apportioned not more than three percentum and not less than one percentum of such revenues. Each state may use the funds apportioned to it under this formulae to pay up to 75 percent of the costs of a hunter safety program and the construction, operation and maintenance of public target ranges, as a part of such programs. These funds may, at the option of the state, also be used for wildlife restoration projects."

Funds may also be available through your state under the Land and Water Conservation Fund administered on the federal level by the Bureau of Outdoor Recreation, U. S. Department of the Interior, Washington, D.C. 20240, James G. Watt, Director. Matching funds can come from many sources. Donation of land needed for a facility is acceptable, providing the site offered has not been used for public recreational purposes. Local units can build the shooting range with their own employees and use such labor as a source of matching funds. Naturally, adequate time records must be maintained for audit purposes and the project must be cleared ahead of time through your state. Projects must be in accord with the comprehensive state-wide outdoor recreation plan, be sponsored by a governmental agency, and meet other state and federal requirements. We suggest you contact the Bureau of Outdoor Recreation at the above address or your State Fish & Game Department. The Superintendent of Documents, U. S. Government Printing Office, Washington, D.C. 20402, has copies of *Digest—Federal Outdoor Recreation Programs and Recreation-Related Environment Programs* available at $1.35 each (stock number 241600055). The *Digest* lists over 290 federal programs of assistance related to outdoor recreation, the major legislative authority under which each program operates, the program's administering agency, and who may apply for assistance and where.